HONOURABLE INSULTS
A Century of Political Invective

Compiled by
GREG KNIGHT MP

Illustrated by
JOHN JENSEN

ARROW BOOKS

Note: In the course of the production of this book there may well have been a number of changes in Members' positions in the Houses of Parliament. While every effort has been made to keep the text up to date, it may not have been possible where a change has taken place between the completion of the manuscript and publication.

Arrow Books Limited
20 Vauxhall Bridge Road, London SW1V 2SA

An imprint of Random Century Group

London Melbourne Sydney Auckland Johannesburg and agencies throughout the world

First published by Robson Books 1990
Arrow edition 1991

Phototypeset by Intype, London
Printed and bound in Great Britain by
Cox & Wyman Ltd, Reading

ISBN 0 09 997230 1

To *my father, for showing me, by example, the art of the gratuitous insult.*

CONTENTS

ACKNOWLEDGEMENTS

The author wishes to thank the following for their help and assistance:

The late Sir John Stradling-Thomas MP, The Lord Cocks, The Lord Brooks of Tremorfa, Rt Hon Michael Heseltine MP, Rt Hon David Mellor QC MP, Donald Thompson MP, Richard Page MP, Terry Dicks MP, Sydney Chapman MP, Andrew MacKay MP, Edwina Currie MP, Nicholas Bennett MP, Robert Rhodes James MP, Tim Devlin MP, Jeremy Hanley MP, Neil Hamilton MP, Janet Ormond, Mark Hayball; and for her help with the manuscript, Teresa Munczel.

The following books contain some excellent political stories, a few of which are recalled here and are acknowledged with grateful thanks:

Upwardly Mobile by Norman Tebbit, published by Weidenfeld and Nicolson, *The Time of My Life* by Denis Healey, published by Michael Joseph, *The Making of a Prime Minister* by Harold Wilson, published by Weidenfeld and Nicolson, *A Sparrow's Flight* by Lord Hailsham, published by Collins, *Life Lines* by Edwina Currie, published by Sidgwick and Jackson, *All the Best* by Edward Koch, published by Simon and Schuster, *The Castle Diaries: 1964–70* by Barbara Castle, published by Weidenfeld and Nicolson, *The Political Diary of Hugh Dalton*, published by Jonathan Cape, *Office Without Power* by Tony Benn MP, published by Hutchinson, *FE* by the Earl of Birkenhead, published by Eyre & Spottiswoode.

INTRODUCTION

The effective insult is something of an art, and usually, but not exclusively, takes a good deal of panache to pull off.

A number of people equate rude behaviour with insulting behaviour. The two are not the same thing. Someone who is vulgar and rude, for whatever reason, is usually embarrassing. Indeed, I have no time for those who think that the effective insult is merely the use of particularly obnoxious or bad language. Such behaviour usually has the effect of insulting the perpetrator by revealing him to be someone of low intelligence and limited vocabulary.

However, the barbed phrase, the piece of quick acid-tongued repartee or some insulting behaviour which humiliates a third party, is a pleasure to behold.

Anyone who has paid the slightest attention to politics over the years will know that one of the main occupations of our elected representatives is insulting each other. Even during a constructive debate or speech, the politician speaking will often take time out to be abusive to his or her opponent.

This is not a twentieth-century phenomenon – politicians have been spewing vitriol at each other through the centuries, and the trend shows no signs of abating.

I have to plead guilty to committing the offence myself frequently. In 1980, when I was serving as a councillor, I became so infuriated with an opposition spokesman that I told him he was 'the perfect cure for anyone with an inferiority complex'. On another occasion, finding myself particularly irritated by the speech of a Socialist councillor, I could not resist accusing him of speaking from a 'position of advanced ignorance'.

Politicians, however, have to be able to take it as well. One of the reasons is that, after mother-in-law jokes, insults about politicians must rank as the most popular with members of the public. A number of years ago, an MP – annoyed at what he regarded as poor service from a hotel – attempted to rectify matters by saying to the receptionist, 'Do you know who I am?' He must have been withered by the reply: 'No, sir, but I will find out – and I will let you know.'

This slight ranks with the reply of Henry Labouchère, who was once confronted with a pompous nobleman who called at the British delegation in St Petersburg and demanded to see the Ambassador. 'Pray, take a chair; he will be here soon,' said Labouchère. 'But, young man, do you not know who I am?' the nobleman replied, reciting his distinctions. 'In that case,' responded Labouchère, 'pray take two chairs.'

In politics it does not pay to have a thin skin. Politicians who are too sensitive and who, at the first criticism, run off to the law courts, have often come a cropper. Apparently what is defamatory to the man in the street may be acceptable invective against a politician. What *is* somewhat surprising is the eagerness of the public to share their insulting stories with the politicians themselves. A well-wisher recently approached me eagerly and posed the question, 'How can you tell when a politician is lying?' Before I was able to utter a word, she added, 'When his lips move.'

One of the most difficult decisions any public figure has to make is when to be insulting and when to exhibit a degree of humility. It was undoubtedly his lack of judgement on this point that prevented the brilliant F E Smith from becoming leader of the Conservative Party – and possibly Prime Minister. Quite simply, he could never curb his tongue and in the process insulted friend and foe alike, many of whom never forgave him.

Unlike some of the people quoted in this book, I have found that in a difficult situation it does, on occasion, pay to be self-deprecating. One Christmas, when I was rather more hirsute than now, I was answering questions at a public meeting when someone from the audience shouted: 'Is it not the case that all politicians are liars?' Although the man was aggressive and rude, I sensed that if I insulted him he would probably gain the sympathy of the audience. I played safe and stroking my beard responded, 'At least you cannot call me a bare-faced one.'

However, this book, as you have undoubtedly guessed from its title, is not concerned with occasions of restraint. It contains for the first time between two covers a collection of some of the most memorable political insults from the past hundred years or so. I have, I admit, been rather liberal in my definition of 'a hundred', deciding to include, for example, a number of insults by Benjamin Disraeli, who died in 1881.

As a Conservative politician, I cannot claim that the contents have been compiled by an impartial observer. So far as the politicians quoted are concerned, I clearly have my favourites, some of whom – quoted in chapter 2 – I am honoured to call personal friends. I have tried to present an equal balance between the parties and have not let my own views stand in the way of the inclusion of a good insult. I have, however, followed certain conventions. Where over the years I have been given information in confidence, I have respected that confidence. Similarly, any information imparted to me in my role as a government Whip will not appear here. Where the insult or invective was delivered in public, in the Commons chamber, or in a committee sitting in open session, then I have regarded it as being in the public domain and appropriate for me to include in this book.

If there is any political message to be found in these pages, it is not simply that politics is a rough business. We all know that. It is that the majority of politicians, consciously or otherwise, are adherents to the aphorism of Gore Vidal: 'It is not enough to succeed – others must fail.'

Greg Knight, MP
House of Commons
September 1990

1
1890–1945: 'Pertinacious Combatism'

OVER THE past hundred years or so, Parliament has witnessed many an occasion when tempers have flared and insults have been thrown across the floor of both Houses in pursuit of some noble aim or objective, or – just as often – in furtherance of some less-than-noble vendetta or settling of old scores.

Benjamin Disraeli died in 1881 but the contributions he made not only to politics but to the art of the parliamentary insult, live on. Time after time, he devastated his opponents with his quick tongue and acidic turn of phrase. When asked to give his opinions of Lord John Russell, he said: 'If a traveller was informed that such a man was Leader of the House of Commons, he might begin to comprehend how the Egyptians worshipped an insect.'

He was no less insulting on Sir Robert Peel: 'He is so vain that he wants to figure in history as the settler of all the great questions; but a parliamentary constitution is not favourable to such ambitions: things must be done by parties, not by persons using parties as tools.' And, as if this was not savage enough, he added for good measure: 'His smile is like the silver fittings on a coffin.'

He hardly had a good word to say about any of his contemporaries. On Lord Liverpool, as Prime Minister: 'The Arch-Mediocrity who presides, rather than rules, over a Cabinet of Mediocrities ... not a statesman, a statemonger ... Peremptory in little questions, the great ones he left open.'

He did not think much even of Britain's capital city, referring to London as 'a modern Babylon'.

His charming of Queen Victoria was well-known and he made no secret of his success with her: 'Everyone likes flattery and when you come to royalty, you should lay it on with a trowel.'

He even opined of his own administration that 'A Conservative government is an organized hypocrisy.'

Among his other most memorable barbs, the following are worthy of note:

'The author who speaks about his own books is almost as bad as the mother who talks about her own children.'

'You know who critics are? The men who have failed in literature and art.'

Of a now-forgotten back-bench MP who was often out of his depth in debates: 'He was distinguished for ignorance; for he had only one idea and that was wrong.'

'It is well known what a middle man is: he is a man who bamboozles one party – and plunders the other.'

'Talk to a man about himself and he will listen for hours.'

During a discussion, a colleague mentioned to Disraeli the humble background of John Bright, the Radical statesman and orator, and pointed out that Bright was entirely a self-made man. 'I know he is,' replied Disraeli, 'and he adores his maker.'

During an election, he was addressing a public meeting and was interrupted by a heckler who shouted, 'Speak up, I can't hear you.' Disraeli responded: 'Truth travels slowly, but it will reach you in time.'

In a heated discussion, he told an MP with whom he disagreed: 'Ignorance never settles a question.'

The Irish political leader Daniel O'Connell made an anti-Semitic remark in his presence. Disraeli flattened him with the response: 'Yes, I am a Jew, and when the ancestors of the right honourable gentlemen were brutal savages in an unknown island, mine were priests in the Temple of Solomon.'

Disraeli was a brilliant House of Commons performer and knew that there are other ways of deflating an opponent than direct verbal insult. At the end of one particular debate, his great rival Gladstone was winding up for the opposition and was making a tremendous speech. His hand crashed repeatedly on the dispatch-box as he assailed Disraeli, who lay back on the Treasury bench, feet on the table, apparently asleep with his top hat tilted forward over his eyes. At every crash of Gladstone's fist, Disraeli's head sank a little lower and lower. Finally, Gladstone came to the climax of his speech – which was very effective – and brought his fist down so hard on the dispatch-box that all the pens and pencils on the table rolled around the surface, some falling on to the floor.

Gladstone sat down and, for a moment, Disraeli made no move. He then took off his hat and slowly got to his feet. He looked around the House and began: 'Mr Speaker, the right honourable gentleman has spoken at great length and with much violence. But the damage can be repaired.' He then very slowly picked up every pen and every pencil from the table and from the floor and put them all back into their holders, while the tension of the House dissolved into laughter. Only after he had completed this task did he begin his own speech, having by then totally destroyed the effect of Gladstone's address.

WILLIAM EWART GLADSTONE outlived Disraeli by some seventeen years to become known as the 'Grand Old Man' of British politics. Frequently criticized for his long and somewhat moralizing speeches, he did not have Disraeli's ready wit and biting turn of phrase but, on occasion, he did deliver broad – but usually rather stoical – abuse. When an admirer told him how much he admired a man who could stand up to his enemies, Gladstone told him: 'Standing up to one's enemies is commendable, but give me the man who can stand up to his friends.'

During one particular debate, Joseph Chamberlain, the Liberal-Unionist politician, made a lengthy attack on Lord Randolph Churchill and concluded with an assault on his political proposals by saying: 'I dare say you have often seen at a bazaar a patchwork quilt brought out for sale which is made up of scraps from old dresses and from left-over garments which the maker has been able to borrow for the purpose . . . that is the programme which Lord Randolph Churchill has placed before you.' Gladstone, however, dismissed Randolph Churchill in a sentence. 'He is like a minute insect which bites without being felt.'

He felt that many politicians did not know when they had overstayed their welcome in office. Although by then an old man himself, he advised a colleague, 'The people should not be too fond of encouraging men to stay too long in their service. They come to be like public singers who begin to sing flat, and they never know when they sing flat, and therefore they do discredit to their former reputation and do not give any pleasure or satisfaction to the ears of those who hear them.'

Although he was a religious man, he was not afraid to attack the Church or its leaders when he believed them to be wrong, proving, if nothing else, that rows between bishops and the government of the day are not new. On the question of Church reform, he told one bishop that his remarks were no more than 'a combination of adroit claptrap and oracular rhodomontade'.

This led to a rather Durham-like response from the Bishop of Ossory, who accused Gladstone's government of being a 'Cabinet of brigands'. For good measure, this ecclesiastical governor added that Gladstone himself was 'a traitor to his Queen, his country and his God'.

After this undignified episode, Gladstone must have felt that the criticisms he later received from the Tories were extremely tame. To be labelled by Her Majesty's Opposition 'a too ardent automedon', a 'casuist hair-splitter', a 'sophistical logic-chopper', and to be criticized by them for his 'joy to force the pace and a tendency to urge his steeds not wisely, but too well', hardly matches the gratuitous vitriol he received at the hand, or rather mouth, of the Christian Church.

In the Commons, Gladstone blasted the Tories for using their favourite weapons in debate: 'Bald assertion, persistent exaggeration, constant misconstruction, and copious, arbitrary and baseless prophecy.'

However, apart from a number of notable exceptions (the Duke of Devonshire's verdict on Gladstone was that he was 'a defeated and discredited statesman') his political opponents appeared to reserve most of their flak for Gladstone's followers, who were accused of being mindless. (An opposition frequently insults loyal government supporters and calls them 'mindless'. It will urge them to exert more influence and speak their mind. When they do, they are called 'disloyal'.)

Of Gladstone's party supporters one of his opponents said, 'If Mr Gladstone was to take it into his head to say "Cock-a-doodle-doo is the highest wisdom," you would find his supporters and the press that support him resounding with "Cock-a-doodle-doo is the highest wisdom." His supporters are phonographs.'

At least one affront perpetuated against Gladstone did not, at the time, become public knowledge — at his request. On 3 March 1894 he resigned as Prime Minister, having served Queen Victoria in ministerial office for a total of some thirty-five years.

Although the Queen was courteous enough to him, relations between the two had not been cordial and he received not one word of thanks for all his years of public service. The Queen's letter in response to his resignation was so curt as to be insulting. Gladstone, who had every right to be bitter, actually asked his family to be most careful to keep quiet his poor personal relationship with the Queen.

SIR CHARLES DILKE is quite forgotten today (he was hardly a household name in his time), but in 1892 he was Member of Parliament for the Forest of Dean and had quite an eye for the ladies. Once, while he was staying at the home of the Tennant family, he made a pass at Laura, the younger sister of Margot Asquith. On his second night in the house, he met her in the passage on her way to bed. Displaying either an appalling ignorance of how to charm a lady, or a monumental ego (or both) he said, 'If you will kiss me, I will give you a signed photograph.' He deserved the reply he got. 'It is awfully good of you, Sir Charles, but I would rather not, for what on earth should I do with a photograph?'

A COLLECTION of photographs would have been of use to Lord Salisbury, thrice Prime Minister, who became rather forgetful towards the end of his career and frequently failed to recognize friends and colleagues.

At a dinner party one evening, he startled his host by asking who was the man sitting opposite to him. The host replied that it was a Mr W H Smith, a member of his Cabinet. Without batting an eyelid, Salisbury said that as Smith sat next to him in Cabinet, he was used to seeing him in profile. It is said that when he resigned from office, King Edward VII gave him a signed photograph of himself. Salisbury, gazing at it, commented,

'Poor Buller.' The King was insulted – but it had not been intentional.

IN 1894, our Prime Minister was Lord Rosebery. He was having difficulty with his Secretary of State for Irish Affairs, Mr John Morley, who refused to make speeches in support of the government of which he was a member. Herbert Henry Asquith (later to be Prime Minister himself) is reported to have tried to console Rosebery with the remark, 'Yes, he is difficult to manage. But at least he's a perfect gentleman.' Lord Rosebery was not impressed and his insult was withering: 'Yes, but I am not sure that he might not be best described as a perfect lady.'

Many of Rosebery's insults, like those of Lord Salisbury, were probably not intended. Lloyd George used to tell of the occasion when there was an important debate in the House of Lords and he heard Rosebery's valet say to him, 'Your grouse is done to a turn.' And as a result, Rosebery disappeared, abandoning the debate.

Sir Henry Campbell-Bannerman, the Liberal Prime Minister, remarked of Lord Rosebery: 'He showed how little political and parliamentary education he had because he thought it was a sufficient defence of any public utterance to say that it was true.'

IT WAS some time in the 1880s when Lord Randolph Churchill was asked if he would stand for Parliament as a Tory Democrat. In those days before selection committees he was able to respond, without affecting his chances of being given a seat, 'To be truthful, I don't know what Tory Democracy is. But I believe it is principally opportunism.'

Lord Curzon, like Rosebery, displayed an arrogance that today would probably lead to demands for his immediate resignation. After visiting an industrial area, Curzon was heard to remark, 'I never knew the lower classes had such white skins.'

When he was at Kedleston House, he was summoned by his valet to the telephone. He was there informed by an official at the Foreign Office that a certain foreign statesman had died suddenly. Curzon rebuked his caller, 'Do you realize that to convey to me this trivial piece of information, you have forced me to walk the length of a mansion the size of Windsor Castle?' To be fair to the noble lord, he was even-handed, being just as insulting to his political boss. When he was asked by Lloyd George to return to London to discuss some important government business, he refused – on the grounds that his house in London was not properly prepared to receive him.

He disliked the Tory Stanley Baldwin, of whom he said, 'Not even a public figure. A man of no experience. And of the utmost inexperience.'

Not surprisingly, he made a number of enemies, amongst them former Prime Minister, Arthur Balfour, who disliked Curzon and often used to gibe at him for living off the fortune of his second wife, Grace. When asked by a colleague whether Curzon would be chosen by the King as Prime Minister, Balfour replied, 'No, he will not. He has lost the hope and the glory – but he still retains the means of Grace.'

Lord Beaverbrook ridiculed him for his extremely pragmatic approach to some issues. 'Curzon has changed sides on almost every issue during his career. He is often undecided whether to desert a sinking ship for one that might not float.'

He was apparently a poor loser. Soon after becoming Prime Minister, Stanley Baldwin met Lord Curzon in Downing Street, and later commented that he had received 'the sort of greeting a corpse would give to an undertaker'.

BALFOUR MAY not have liked Curzon, but he had even less time for Liberal Prime Minister Henry Campbell-Bannerman. He called him 'a mere cork, dancing on a current which he cannot control'.

When told by a colleague that he was being long-winded and that he should 'be brief, like Asquith', Balfour appeared unconcerned, and retorted: 'Asquith's lucidity of style is a positive disadvantage when one has nothing to say.'

He dismissed one MP's fervour for reform with the remark that it was 'unfortunate, considering that enthusiasm moves the world, that so few enthusiasts can be trusted to speak the truth'.

He died in 1930 and if today his achievements are forgotten by all but the most ardent historian, he did at least utter one *bon mot*, reportedly on his death-bed, which is worth repeating. He pondered, 'If there is no future life, this world is a bad joke; but whose joke?'

LORD ACTON did not think much of the statesmen of the time, commenting: 'Power tends to corrupt and absolute power corrupts absolutely. Great men are almost always bad men.'

MENTION THE name of F E Smith or, as he was later to become, Lord Birkenhead, and today few people will know who you are talking about. It is a fact of life that unless a politician rises to become Prime Minister, or is involved in a scandal, his memory soon fades in the public mind. It is almost certain that the name of the relatively junior minister Jack Profumo will still be remembered for many generations to come, whereas the Earl of Birkenhead, a contemporary of Winston Churchill and regarded in his day as 'the brainiest man in Britain', is now largely forgotten.

Frederick Edwin Smith was not only brainy. He was one of the most brilliant advocates of all time. He became perhaps the most effective orator speaking in the Conservative Party's cause almost immediately he entered Parliament.

His early rise through the party's ranks was meteoric. Only a few years after his election to the Commons, he was made a Privy Councillor; shortly afterwards he became Solicitor General, then Attorney General, and then joined the Cabinet as Lord Chancellor. Many of his contemporaries felt that, if it had not been for his acidic tongue and his readiness to brush aside the opinions of others with an insult, he might well have become Prime Minister. Lord Beaverbrook summed up the widely held view of most of Smith's contemporaries when he said, 'His chief enemy has always been his own biting and witty tongue, which spares no man.'

It was in 1906 that F E, as he was widely known, was first elected as Conservative MP for Birkenhead. His maiden speech was brilliant. Even then, in his first parliamentary year, his insults were already legend. He continued to practise as a barrister and relished insulting a county court judge called Willis, whom he regarded as sanctimonious and patronizing.

When Smith was appearing in a court case for a company which was being sued for injuries to a youth who had been run over, Judge Willis suggested that the young man, when giving evidence, be put on a chair so the jury could see him. 'Perhaps your honour would like to have the boy passed round the jury,' suggested F E. The judge, regarding the remark as improper, asked, 'Mr Smith, have you ever heard of a saying by Bacon that youth and discretion are ill-wed companions?'

'Yes, I have, your honour. Has your honour ever heard of a saying by Bacon that a much-talking judge is like an ill-tuned cymbal?' The insults continued until the judge declared angrily, 'You are extremely offensive, young man.' And F E responded: 'As a matter of fact, we both are; the only difference between us is that I am trying to be and you can't help it.'

The same judge, on another occasion, was involved in a long legal wrangle with Smith. Finally coming to the end of his patience he said: 'What do you suppose I am on the bench for, Mr Smith?' F E responded, 'It is not for me, your honour, to attempt to fathom the inscrutable workings of Providence.'

During the early part of his legal career, and before he entered politics, Smith was appointed Secretary to the National Church League, a favourite cause of Lady Wimborne. He took offices for the League and erected a brass plate on the door announcing 'Lady Wimbourne's League'. Lady Wimborne came up to Liverpool to see how the cause was progressing, and looked aghast at the misspelling. 'How would you like it, Mr Smith, if I were to spell your name wrong on a plate?' F E answered without hesitation: 'My dear lady, there is scarcely any alteration that you could make to it which would not add to its distinction.' This was a brave response. She sacked him the next day.

No one was spared his rude, abrupt and insulting behaviour, not even his wife. Once, when he'd spent some time in London working on a legal case, he arrived late at his local station to find that she had forgotten to send a carriage to collect him. The railway was some three miles from his house and his wife, realizing her error too late, had no option but to await his return home.

At last she heard the door open and F E entered, followed by a filthy tramp who was carrying his baggage. The tramp smelled appalling. 'Sit down, my dear sir,' F E said, and then turned upon his wife. 'Had it not been for the courtesy of this gentleman, I should have been compelled to carry this heavy luggage all the way from the station myself. Will you kindly give him some food and drink?' According to F E's son, this event silenced Mrs Smith of all argument for nearly six months.

In the late 1920s, the Liberal Dingle Foot was due to address the Oxford Union. Also due to address this body was F E Smith. Dingle Foot unwisely chose an insulting anecdote to needle Smith. He said there were two brilliant undergraduates, the Liberal John Simon and F E Smith, and they were talking together in their undergraduate days and agreeing that, as they were both of such outstanding ability, one or the other must certainly become Prime Minister one day, and therefore they could not afford to remain in the same political party. Dingle Foot went on to relate how they tossed a coin as to which should remain a Liberal, and F E Smith lost.

In response, F E Smith said: 'That anecdote bears all the characteristics of a Liberal pleasantry. In the first place, it is a lie. In the second place, it is not funny. In the third place, it is calculated to give offence – not to myself, of course, because it is a matter of supreme indifference to me what my young friend may say or think. But think of the pain it will cause when I go back to Westminster and recount it to my old friend and colleague, Sir John Simon.'

His colleagues at Westminster delighted in his brilliant repartee, but he sometimes made an uneasy companion as they never knew when an insult was heading their way.

On his way to the House of Lords from his London home, F E, who had always been a Tory, was fond of calling at the National Liberal Club to use their lavatory. This practice continued for a number of months until one day the doorman became rather suspicious and stopped Smith as he left the WC. 'Excuse me, sir, are you a member?' he enquired.

Smith's response was typical: 'Good gracious, don't tell me that this place is a club,' he snapped. 'I thought it was a public lavatory.'

Among his most memorable sayings are the following:

On political morality: 'To say what is not is that by which one-third cajoles the other two-thirds.'

When asked if the Conservative Party should change its leader just before a general election: 'We must not swap donkeys crossing the stream.'

Of Winston Churchill: 'He is a man of simple tastes – he's always prepared to put up with the best of everything.' And: 'Winston has devoted the best years of his life to preparing his impromptu speeches.'

On the Liberal Government's proposals to reform the House of Lords: 'The truth is that the Liberals do not want to abolish the House of Lords when it opposes the people – but wish to abolish the people when they oppose the Liberal Party.'

On the Liberal landslide in 1906: 'These Liberals came floating into Parliament like corks on the top of a dirty wave.'

Showing his contempt for Lord Salisbury and Lord Selborne he called them 'Dolly Sisters'.

On death: 'A man's works should be remembered and his life forgotten.'

On the Liberal Government: 'The government has turned its back on the country, and now has the impertinence to claim the country is behind it.'

Of the Cabinet in 1923: 'Incompetent, they all have second-class brains.'

On Stanley Baldwin: 'He is a little half-wit who has gone mad. He simply takes one jump in the dark, looks around, and then takes another.'

Of the second Labour government: 'I have not a high opinion either of their intellect or of their experience.'

On Lord Rothermere: 'Such pertinacious combatism.'

In the 1920s, on the then Mr Wedgwood-Benn (later Viscount Stansgate, father of Tony Benn), 'He is the world's best-known political featherweight.'

Of Mr A J Cook, the miners' leader at the time of the General Strike: 'He suffers from a somewhat neurotic and hysterical temperament. He has a small but not a very considerable gift as a demagogue. Indeed, even in this direction, his foaming but ungrammatical periods not infrequently overtax his physical strength. The heady wine of Russia proved too strong for an intelligence both shallow and febrile.'

And his view of the General Strike leaders: 'The strike was not directed at the mine owners. It was directed against the government, because the government was determined to pay no further subsidy to the coal industry. It was, therefore, an attempt by a body of men who had no representative capacity, to dictate to Parliament. They could easily, if things had gone well, have been persuaded to become members of the first English Soviet.'

Of J B Priestley: 'The conversations in his novels may be true to life, but they are at times remote from art. Mr Priestley's pages, like Prohibition beer, are only ten per cent inspired.'

On writer Robert Graves: 'He wrote much that is excellent, much that is mediocre and much that is so worthless as to prejudice the value of the rest.'

And his view of the writer H G Wells: 'He dithers and blathers about a better world, and paints a stupid and false picture of the General Strike.'

During the fierce debates on the Liberals' controversial budget after their landslide victory, when some Liberals had spoken of 'a revolution', Smith responded bitingly: 'I don't wish to be offensive, but the Liberals opposite are not the kind of stuff of which revolutionaries are made. The respectable and benign countenances facing me are ill-suited to the red cap of revolution. Tea-meetings are more in their line.'

In 1911, when the Tories were in opposition, there was something of an upset when it became clear to Arthur Balfour, their Leader, that Asquith, Liberal Prime Minister, was intending to make a Privy Councillor of F E Smith, who had not been on Balfour's list submitted to the government, in place of Hayes Fisher, who had.

Balfour, who respected Smith but did not like him, decided to tell F E that he was writing to the Prime Minister to ask that Smith should not be awarded the honour, but that it should go to Hayes Fisher as originally planned. F E might have accepted this without complaint, had it not been for a letter sent by a Mr Sandars, who was Balfour's assistant, pointing out to Smith that he was a young man who could afford to wait for the honour and adding, somewhat unwisely, that 'in years to come your little boy would be proud of his father for making such a sacrifice'. Such an incautious remark was bound to lead to some hot words of insult from F E. He wrote back: 'My little boy is only four years old, but if I thought that he was such a bloody little fool as to be proud of his father for behaving in such an asinine manner, I should indeed despair of him.' The result did have a happy ending in that Asquith compromised in the end, and both F E Smith and Hayes Fisher became Privy Councillors. However, Smith's outburst in his letter to Sandars led to continuing coolness between him and Balfour who wrote to ask F E if he intended to take his seat (then reserved by custom for a Privy Councillor) on the opposition front bench but pointedly, however, did not invite him to do so.

Smith publicly disagreed with his own party's tactics in 1909. He said later: 'Compared with our modern visitations, the 1909 Budget seems an almost harmless measure, hardly more than a gentle flick of the whip over the back of the now raw-flayed taxpayer. But it changed the political face of England. The leaders of the Conservative Party threw away every trump they held by the stupidity with which they played their cards. And they finished off with a revoke. Instead of accepting the Budget and allowing it to collapse, as it would inevitably have done under the weight of its own faults, the Peers threw it out giving to Mr Lloyd George the cry of 'the Peers against the People'. The Lords then capped their first folly – the rejection of the Budget – by allowing the Parliament Act to pass. When they should have yielded they have been obstinate; when they should have been firm they surrendered.'

Chastising the Liberal government in 1912 for their proposals for Irish Home Rule, he accused them of being optimists, but went on: 'An optimist is an admirable character if it means a person who exhibits a fortitude, or even a cheerful recklessness, in the face of his own danger. It is a much less admirable character if it merely means one who retains cheerfulness before the prospect of danger to others.'

It was always an unwise move to try to get the better of Smith in debate. Once a Liberal MP sarcastically and sneeringly asked him why he was speaking in favour of the Corn Production Bill, alleging that he knew nothing about it. Smith flattened him with the response: 'I am one of the few who have attempted to take part in this debate wholly uncontaminated by any expert knowledge of agriculture.'

He did not think much of the Duke of Northumberland's campaign on the Irish Treaty in 1921, for he commented, 'The noble Duke has been stalking the country for the last six months, avoiding some processes of labour by always delivering the same speech. In his mind every soldier is a superman and every politician is either a rogue or a fool.'

Horatio Bottomley, the Liberal politician, was a colourful but less than honest character who was an acquaintance of F E's. He lacked Smith's style in the art of the parliamentary insult, his manner being rather obvious and heavy-handed. Of Germans living in Britain just after the outbreak of the First World War, he had said, 'I call for a vendetta – a vendetta against every German in Britain. You cannot naturalize an unnatural beast – a human abortion – a hellish freak. But you can exterminate him. And now the time has come.' When it was announced that Smith was going to be made Lord Chancellor, Bottomley congratulated F E and added: 'I shouldn't have been surprised to hear that you'd also been made Archbishop of Canterbury.'

'If I had,' replied F E, 'I should have asked you to come to my installation.'

'That's damned nice of you,' said Bottomley.

'Not at all,' Smith replied, 'I should have needed a crook.'

The Railwaymen's leader, Jimmy Thomas, was elected as an MP in 1910. Just after his election, and before he had learnt his way around the House of Commons, he happened to ask F E the way to the lavatory. Smith's response was typical. 'Down the corridor, first right, first left and down the stairs', Smith told him. 'Then you'll see a door marked "gentlemen", but don't let that deter you.'

After he became Lord Chancellor, F E, ennobled as Lord Birkenhead, came into close contact with King George V. Although Smith admired the King, and the way that he discharged his duties, it appears that His Majesty regarded his new Lord Chancellor with mixed feelings. Smith's flamboyance did not always go down well at the Palace, where he was regarded as somewhat unpredictable. Things came to a head during negotiations for the Irish Treaty in 1921. Smith, as Lord Chancellor, was photographed arriving for a meeting at Number 10 Downing Street wearing a grey and rather flashy suit with a soft felt hat, instead of the morning dress which was *de rigueur* at that time. On the King's instructions, Lord Stamfordham wrote to the Lord Chancellor's secretary, Sir Claud Schuster, to point out the King's displeasure at Smith's somewhat bohemian appearance. The letter came to the attention of Smith, and his temper was roused.

His reply to Lord Stamfordham contains equal measure of insult and sarcasm: 'It seems incongruous in these anxious days to pursue grave controversy in the matter referred to. On the morning in question, I came up from the country where I had no silk hat and my train did not arrive in time to enable me to go home before the conference. It will not, I think, be suggested that it would have been proper to arrive late at the conference in order to make good the defect in my equipment! The measure of my shortcoming, therefore, is that I did not remember to take a silk hat with me when I left London three days earlier.'

He went on: 'We must hope that I shall be able to avoid such lapses in the future. And after all, in days far more formal than ours, it was never the custom to appraise the adequacy or dignity of Lord Chancellors in terms of headgear.' The King, it was later reported, regarded the letter as 'very rude' and was extremely disgruntled by Smith's insulting response.

After he had ceased to be Lord Chancellor, Smith toured America where he met President Woodrow Wilson. He was not particularly impressed with the President and observed, 'President Wilson indeed came to office with a noble message of hope, but unhappily in the sequel, hope proved to be his main equipment.' During a meeting he had with the President, he became irritated when asked by an official to back out of the President's presence. He was also annoyed that he was unable to get President Wilson to discuss any serious topic. Smith's questions were blandly side-stepped by the President, who rambled on at length about historical matters in the seventeenth century. At last the President inquired of Smith, 'And what in your opinion is the trend of the modern English undergraduate?'

'Steadily towards women and drink,' replied the exasperated Smith.

Although he regarded Lloyd George as a great statesman, this did not stop F E severely criticizing him when he believed he had made a mistake: 'Only the certitude that he would never be called upon to prove his claim, can have permitted him, at the last general election, to declare that he could cure unemployment in a year without the expenditure of public money.'

Later, for a period of nearly five years, Smith served as Secretary of State for India. He had some harsh words to say about those whom he came into contact with. Of Indian politicians: 'They are mostly educated in the school of that Western learning which they pretend so much to despise.' Of the Indian press he said: 'The most illiterate press in the world . . . run by the most superficial hotheads in the world.' Of those Indian politicians seeking home rule: 'To judge by the speeches which are made by old Harrow boys and members of the Inns of Court, who ought to despise Western civilization so much that they would not condescend to speak its language, but who owe their own capacity for mischief to the education which they have derived from the West, they have reached the conclusion that if the despised English left India tomorrow, a happy and united country would acclaim the political rebirth of a great subcontinent. The greatest proof of the incompetence of those leaders, who owe their language, their science, and their sophisticated commercial system to the West, is that they have completely failed to realize what would happen to India if the British Raj was withdrawn. It is a commonplace that if Great Britain left India tomorrow, India would dissolve into an anarchy.'

When assailed by a constituent who appeared to despise politicians generally, he replied: 'Every voter is, to some extent, a politician; every man who can argue is a lawyer in embryo. The public cannot forgive their superiors.'

And his view of Soviet Russia: 'They are a semi-civilized people whose national characteristics of cruelty and a disregard for human life must be numbered among their traits.'

Of the Liberal decline in the early part of this century he said: 'The stupid Cobdenite mind of the moribund Liberal Party never perceived the truth. In all the fundamentals of life – alike in foreign and domestic policy – Liberals have been wrong.'

Once he was addressing an election meeting in his constituency and he said to the assembled crowd: 'Now I shall tell you what the government has done for all of you.'

At this point, a woman in the audience yelled 'nothing!'

'My dear lady,' said F E, 'The light in this hall is so dim as to prevent a clear sight of your undoubted charms, so I am unable to say with certainty whether you are a virgin, a widow, or a matron, but in any case, I will guarantee to prove that you are wrong. If you are a young virgin, we have given you the vote; if you are a wife, we have increased employment and reduced the cost of living; if you are a widow, we have given you a pension – and if you are none of these, but are foolish enough to be a tea drinker, we have reduced the tax on sugar.'

Friend and foe alike marvelled at his spontaneity in debate. Smith knew this was his strong point and on more than one occasion when he had delivered an impromptu speech, without a single note, he would say: 'I always feel best when I am on the unpinioned wing.'

At another election meeting, he was addressing a crowd on the subject of free trade when a heckler shouted 'You want to tax my food.' F E responded 'No, Sir – there is no proposal to put a tax on thistles.'

Later, when he was arguing the benefits of tariff reform, someone shouted 'Rats'. F E responded 'You are thinking of your larder under free trade.'

At a rally in Liverpool, he asked his audience: 'Is anyone better off now because of the land taxes?' Although the majority of the audience shouted 'No', one hostile heckler yelled 'Yes'. F E crushed him with: 'The gentleman who said "yes" must be a solicitor.'

Towards the end of his life he again turned his acid tongue on members of his own party. He described Conservative right-wingers as 'a set of political half-wits' and said of the Labour Party: 'The Socialist movement in England has never been remarkable for the possession of first-class brains.'

His last view of William Gladstone was: 'He gripped audiences by the fire and earnestness of his address, but his speeches, today, are for the most part unreadable.'

On Leon Trotsky: 'His abilities seem to consist chiefly in vigorous abuse of the people who disagree with him – say ninety-nine out of every hundred people in every country and political party in the world.'

It was a combination of his acidic tongue and his own devilish sense of humour that made him as many enemies as friends. When he was attending a luncheon in Swansea to mark the opening of the new town hall there, he found himself sitting next to the Prince of Wales. They both had to sit through a long-winded speech by the Mayor, which seemed never-ending. F E picked up a menu card, wrote a few words on the back, and asked the toastmaster to give it to the speaker. Shortly after he had done this, the Mayor made some very brief closing remarks and sat down. The Prince of Wales, who had noticed the incident asked F E what he had written. 'Oh, nothing much', Smith replied, 'I just told him his fly buttons were undone.'

During the First World War, he generously gave up his London house to the American Red Cross. On booking into a hotel with his wife, he noticed that the guest immediately before him was the clan chief Cameron of Lochiel, who had signed the hotel register simply 'Lochiel and Lady Cameron.' Not to be outdone by this, F E promptly wrote on the next line '32 Grosvenor Gardens and Mrs Smith.'

Smith was probably the only politician in whose presence Churchill felt somewhat inferior. Winston, who himself had a vicious turn of insult, would remain silent if admonished by Smith. On one occasion, F E said to Churchill: 'Shut up Winston. You have said enough. It's not as if you've got a pretty voice.' To the amazement of all present, Churchill fell silent for the rest of the evening.

Churchill himself later commented: 'People were afraid of him and of what he would say. Even I, who knew him so well, refrained from pushing ding-dong talk too far when others were present, lest friendship should be endangered.'

Smith's favourite drink was whisky and towards the end, his tipple was like petrol to an engine, but as one historian has commented 'In the end the petrol won'.

Once, when he found himself seated at a dinner next to a rather pompous woman who introduced herself as 'Mrs Porter-Porter, with a hyphen.' F E, ordering himself another drink, loftily replied that he was 'Mr Whisky-Whisky, with a syphon.'

Paying generous tribute to his friend after his death, Churchill said: 'I never separated from him without having learnt something. His Counsel was invaluable. He was a man of the world; man of affairs; master of the law; adept at the written or spoken word, but he seemed to have a double dose of human nature. He burned all his candles at both ends.'

At the time of his untimely death in 1930, at the age of fifty-eight, it could not be denied that he had had a distinguished career both at the bar and in politics. However, looking over his public life, one cannot help feeling something of a sense of waste. His acid tongue undoubtedly contributed more 'honourable insults' than anyone else over the past hundred years. Indeed, Smith's tongue was a lethal weapon, which unfortunately he could not control. It would turn on friend and foe alike with the result that he made far too many enemies to allow him to achieve the highest office in the land. Towards the end of his career, it is clear that he had become bored by serving with and under lesser intellects than his own.

He could undoubtedly have been Prime Minister, except that he did not suffer fools *at all* – for a politician a serious defect – and his insults were directed just too often at his friends and colleagues. Bonar Law described the man accurately when he said, 'It would have been easier for him to keep a live coal in his mouth than a witty saying.' Nancy Astor, Britain's first woman MP to take her seat, also caught Smith's mood when she said, 'The penalty of success is to be bored by people who used to snub you.'

AS WE have seen, many of the contemporaries of Lloyd George were biting in their criticism of the fiery Welshman. Of course, as with many of the political insults thrown today, a good number of these barbs were largely unjustified.

The imminence of a general election, and the desire to impress the electorate or the House does tend to add an acerbic tinge to a politician's vocabulary. It was the late Reginald Maudling who said in the mid-1970s, 'As an election approaches, there is a temptation on both sides to maximize the differences between us and to try to escalate the condemnation of our opponents. That, in the nature of things, is inevitable, but it does not serve the public interest.' In a democracy, no doubt, so it always will be.

David Lloyd George proved to be an excellent premier, leading Britain with courage and tenacity through the First World War. Today, however, it is the denigrating abuse thrown either at or by him that is chiefly remembered. For if he received his fair share of abuse, he certainly dished it out as well. He was scathing, if rather coarse, about politician Herbert Samuel, about whom he said, 'When they circumcised him they threw away the wrong bit.'

Of Tory Prime Minister Neville Chamberlain he said: 'He saw foreign policy through the wrong end of a municipal drainpipe.' And commenting on Irish statesman Eamon De Valera: 'He is like trying to pick up mercury with a fork.' (To which De Valera, when told, responded: 'Why doesn't he try a spoon?')

Michael Collins, former Minister of Finance in Eire, later described Lloyd George as: 'Someone with a great deal of craft in his political methods. He would, however, sell his nearest and dearest for political prestige.'

Replying to the Duke of Buccleuch's allegation that the heavy taxation proposed in the 1909 budget would prevent him paying his subscription to his local football club, Lloyd George said: 'A fully equipped Duke costs as much to keep up as two Dreadnoughts; and they are just as great a terror and they last longer.'

Among the most memorable of his brief witticisms are the following:

On Ramsay MacDonald: 'He has sufficient conscience to bother him – but not enough to keep him straight.'

The Welsh Wizard
Conjures with words.

VOTE
HEROES
FIT
LAND
FOR
ME

On the House of Commons: 'To anyone with politics in his blood, this place is like a pub to a drunkard.'

On French Prime Minister Raymond Poincaré: 'Poincaré knows everything and understands nothing – Briand understands everything and knows nothing.'

Commenting on his own party: 'Liberalism is in an advanced state of creeping paralysis. The world is whirling towards a catastrophe and the Liberal Party stands staring on.'

On the 1905 Tory government: 'They died with their drawn salaries in their hands.'

Of Lord Kitchener, during his period as War Minister: 'One of those revolting lighthouses which radiate momentary gleams of revealing light and then suddenly relapse into complete darkness. There are no intermediate stages.'

Of Field Marshal Haig: 'He's brilliant – to the top of his boots.'

His view on Arthur Balfour's impact on history: 'It is no more than the whiff of scent on a lady's handkerchief.'

On F E Smith: 'A man with the vision of an eagle – with a blind spot in his eye.'

And expressing his view of Lord Derby: 'A harpooned walrus.'

Most of his barbs were, understandably, directed at his political opponents but he would occasionally take a verbal swipe at his colleagues. Of his then fellow Liberal Winston Churchill, he opined: 'He has half a dozen solutions to any problem and one of them is right – but the trouble is he does not know which it is.'

Although it is clear that he had some respect for Churchill, Lloyd George thought very little of Lord Gladstone, the son of the former Prime Minister, describing him as: 'A pygmy posturing before the footlights in the road of a giant.' On a subsequent occasion he lambasted 'Gladstone Junior', calling him 'the best living embodiment of the Liberal doctrine that quality is not hereditary.'

One of the few things that he shared with Stanley Baldwin was a detestation of Lord Northcliffe. He described him as 'A volatile creature, so prone to hop from one political position to another that he could rightly be compared to a flea.'

Indeed, where Northcliffe was concerned, Lloyd George seemed to have a penchant for insect metaphors. On a later occasion, he said of him: 'An alliance with him is like going for a walk with a grasshopper.'

THE FORMER Liberal Prime Minister, Herbert Henry Asquith, provided a fitting epitaph for Bonar Law as he left Westminster Abbey after his funeral. His old enemy had been Prime Minister for only twenty-nine weeks, causing Asquith to comment, 'It is fitting that we should have buried the Unknown Prime Minister by the side of the Unknown Soldier.' Margot Asquith, Asquith's wife, would have probably made a better Prime Minister than her husband, if her quick-witted insulting remarks are anything to go by. Of Winston Churchill she said, 'He would kill his own mother just so that he could use her skin to make a drum to beat his own praises.'

She did not think much of Lloyd George either, commenting, 'He could not see a belt without hitting below it.' Even those she admired did not escape completely unscathed. When she was asked for her views on F E Smith she conceded that he was 'very clever', but went on to add 'but his brains go to his head'.

During a visit to America, she visited Hollywood, where she was introduced to the actress Jean Harlow who asked about the pronunciation of Margot, her Christian name. Mrs Asquith replied 'The T is silent — as in Harlow.'

She respected the intellect of the Labour politician Sir Stafford Cripps, but not his judgement, venturing to say to a colleague of her husband, 'Sir Stafford has a brilliant mind – until it is made up.'

Even her own husband did not escape her acid tongue. She said publicly of him: 'His modesty amounts to a deformity.'

STANLEY BALDWIN had no doubt about where he stood in politics. The Conservative Prime Minister openly admitted on more than one occasion that he was more interested in political success than the pursuit of any particular creed. He boasted, 'I would rather be an opportunist and float, than go to the bottom with my principles around my neck.'

Understandably, this led to a good deal of criticism of him from those who saw him as dishonourable. He was, however, a fighter and gave as good as he got. After being attacked in the newspapers, he said of two press barons, Lords Beaverbrook and Rothermere, 'What the proprietorship of these papers is aiming at is power and power without responsibility – the prerogative of the harlot throughout the ages.'

The hate-hate relationship with Beaverbrook continued, with the latter subsequently commenting on Baldwin: 'His successive attempts to find a policy remind me of the chorus of a third-rate review. His evasions reappear in different scenes and in new dresses, and every time they dance with renewed and despairing vigour. But it is the same old jig.'

Lloyd George, on more than one occasion, felt the lash of Baldwin's tongue; his most memorable insult against the Liberal leader was, 'He spent his whole life in plastering together the true and the false, and therefrom manufacturing the plausible.'

He could on occasion be amusing as well as insulting.

Asquith

At the time of Baldwin's premiership, there was an MP for Leith in Scotland named Ernest Brown, who had a large, booming voice. One day he was talking in the Lobby to some of his constituents and his voice could be heard in the Chamber. Baldwin turned to his PPS and asked him what the noise was, to be told, 'It's only Ernest Brown talking to his constituents.'

'Why can't he use the telephone?' riposted Baldwin.

PRESS MAGNATE Beaverbrook clearly had respect for the talents of Winston Churchill, but it did not stop him from commenting in print: 'Winston, on top of the wave, has in him the stuff of which tyrants are made.'

His view of Lloyd George was similar to his feelings about Baldwin, and he was prompted to remark of the Welshman, 'He does not care in which direction the car is travelling, so long as he remains in the driving seat.'

On F E Smith he was less acerbic: 'He was a man of supreme intellectual ability with an amazing power of making mistakes in the minor affairs of life. He was always the worst judge of his own affairs and the best judge of other people's. He was a man without nerves, physically brave to a point of recklessness.'

He said of his one-time friend, MP Tom Driberg: 'He is driven by malice and hatred. Man has been falling ever since the birth of Adam, but never in the whole course of human history has any man fallen quite so low as Driberg.'

Like all pressmen, he could be gratuitously coarse. He was 'engaged' in the lavatory when an employee sought him out. 'You will have to wait,' the man was told. 'I can only deal with one shit at a time.'

LEO AMERY, the former Conservative MP, will long be remembered for repeating an insult which again

44

caught the mood of the times. Many Conservatives were anxious for a change in direction by their own government, which had been trying to appease Hitler. In a speech attacking Neville Chamberlain in 1940, Amery echoed Oliver Cromwell's speech of January 1654 to the Rump Parliament: 'You have sat too long for any good you have been doing. Depart, I say, and let us have done with you. In the name of God, go!'

A few years earlier, he had effectively criticized the Liberal premier, Asquith, with a hard-hitting attack, which concluded: 'He combines unrivalled gifts of parliamentary leadership with a complete incapacity to face facts or to come to any decision upon them. It would be futile to attempt to strip off the outer integument of debating points in order to get to the real Mr Asquith underneath. There is no such person. For twenty years, he has held a season ticket on the line of least resistance, and has gone wherever the train of events has carried him, lucidly justifying his position at whatever point he has happened to find himself.'

Meanwhile, Lady Cunard's views on Asquith were rather more terse and less colourful: 'Herbert Asquith is black and wicked and has only a nodding acquaintance with the truth.'

SIR ALAN (A P) Herbert, the Independent Member of Parliament and humorous English writer said of the British party system, 'I am sure that the party system is right and necessary. All cannot be fly-halves; there must be a scrum.'

When he was approached by a colleague who referred to his own twenty-five years of blissfully happy married life, Sir Alan replied, 'The conception of two people living together for twenty-five years without having a cross word between them suggests a lack of spirit only to be admired in sheep.'

VICTORIAN IRISH MP Daniel O'Connell, commenting on Lord Alvanley: 'He is a bloated buffoon.'

DURING A row to provide free school meals, the opposition to the measure led the then Liberal MP for Liverpool, Major Seely, to say of his opponents: 'The committee have seen a good deal this evening of the opposition of the overfed members to the underfed child.'

POLITICIANS OF all parties, from all ages, would probably not find any disagreement with the comments of Sir Ernest Benn when he said, 'Politics is the art of looking for trouble, finding it everywhere, diagnosing it wrongly, and applying unsuitable remedies.'

CLEMENT ATTLEE was probably the most self-effacing and laconic Prime Minister of all time. The newsreel film of him that exists shows him as an apparently shy and quiet man who would certainly never set the world on fire with his oratory, his talents lying in the field of administration and of managing to keep the potentially warring elements of the Labour Party together. This view has been confirmed by one former member of his cabinet, Harold now Lord Wilson, who has described him as managing his government in the style of a secondary school headmaster: efficiently but without flair. He did, however, occasionally, make a number of caustic comments worthy of note.

Despite these occasional moments of spark Attlee had – and has – an extremely negative public image. Perhaps this is partly due to the fact in his time he was the butt-end of many of Churchill's taunts. ('An empty taxi cab drew up at the House of Commons and Clement Attlee got out.')

He nevertheless did have a waspish, if terse, turn of insult. Just after the Second World War, when Churchill had returned to the opposition benches, Attlee was dealing with a particular issue when Churchill interrupted to say that the matter had been brought up several times by him in the wartime Cabinet of which he was a member. Attlee responded: 'I must remind the right honourable gentleman that a monologue is not a decision.'

He was later to say of Churchill, 'The trouble with Winston is that he nails his trousers to the mast and can't climb down.'

Attlee was deeply insulting about his predecessor, Ramsay MacDonald, accusing him of having no constructive ideas: 'During his second period in office, I noticed his increasing vanity and snobbery. He perpetrated the greatest betrayal in the political history of Britain.'

He developed a loathing for MacDonald which can only exist between former political friends, going on to add: 'He gradually declined. His speeches became increasingly incoherent and for the last years of his life, he was only a melancholy passenger in the Conservative ship.' (In a rather prophetic remark about himself MacDonald, when Labour leader, had said: 'I am fit, but with a feeling of coming flop.')

Attlee's view of the former Labour Chancellor of the Exchequer, Philip Snowden, was less harsh: 'He fell completely under the spell of orthodox finance and the influence of the governor of the Bank of England. He clung obstinately to the gold standard, while he had a fanatical devotion to free trade.'

Contemporaries of Attlee often referred to his habit of sitting slouched on the government front bench apparently concentrating on his notes, whereas in fact, he would be 'doodling' on the Commons order paper – and taking little interest in the debate – until someone raised a point which he wished to challenge. Then he would jump to his feet and, in his laconic headmaster's style, intervene. Once, when one of his back-benchers was pondering whether or not the 'Middle' East should not really be called the 'Near' East, Attlee jumped to the dispatch-box and said: 'It all depends where you start from.'

Among his terse critical comments, the following are of note:

Of Stafford Cripps: 'He was not a good judge of men, nor had he enough experience to temper his enthusiasm. He was a political goose.'

Of his own party: 'The Labour Party contains a very large pacifist element. In the early days socialist pacifism was a product of the optimistic Victorian era when the British Navy ruled the seas.'

Of Herbert Morrison (after hearing that he wished to be Party leader): 'I never knew that the poor little man was so full of seething ambition.'

And when, during the 1950 election, a number of Conservative-Liberal coalitions in some of the constituencies produced Labour defeats, he said of the coalitionists: 'How do I know what they stand for? They are liquorice allsorts.'

ERNEST BEVIN, the Foreign Secretary in Attlee's government, was not a good Commons performer. Launching into a speech his sentences began but never ended, and Bevin usually finished as breathless and exhausted as all those who had been listening to him.

His strong point was his rapport with working men and his contacts with the trade unions. He had tremendous support in the country and did help Britain to secure Marshall Aid after the war. He approached his parliamentary speeches – as he did his negotiations with foreign countries – rather like a trade union meeting.

When he was asked on a particular subject to 'keep an open mind' he retorted that 'an open mind is like an open sewer'. To his officials' advice that there was a 'gentleman's agreement' on a matter, he responded, 'If there is, show me the gentleman!' He was never known for his patience and, on one occasion when he was reporting to the House of Commons following a conference he'd attended in Moscow, he apologized for boring MPs, and added, 'I know what it's like – I've had six weeks of it.'

THE ISSUE of defence has always been the Achilles' heel of the British Labour Party. As long ago as 1936, the Australian politician Sir Robert Menzies, later to be that country's Prime Minister, said bitingly to Stafford Cripps, 'Defence policy? I did not know that you had one. I now observe that Labour are all for sanctions imposed by the League of Nations and that you will fully support them; and that if this leads to hostilities, you will wage war with bows and arrows.'

SIR OSWALD MOSLEY, who was the founder of the British Union of Fascists, was a mob orator who could excite crowds to frenzy not so much by the quality of his speeches as by his inflammatory language. As he served for a time as an MP he qualifies for inclusion in this book. His turn of phrase was basic in the extreme. When insulting his opponents he made quite clear what his approach was going to be. He told them, 'The only methods we shall employ will be English ones. We shall rely on the good old English fist.'

And, rather in the same vein, he pronounced: 'War is to man what childbirth is to woman.'

AT ABOUT the same time as Mosley was strutting around, another fascist, the Italian dictator Benito Mussolini, was taking a similar line. He was not afraid to insult his own people and said, 'The Italian race is a race of sheep.' Shortly afterwards he commented, 'To make a people great, it is necessary to send them to battle, even if you have to kick them in the pants.'

Within a few months, many British MPs would agree with Mussolini's comments about the need to force the Italians to fight. During the Second World War, it became a popular gibe at Westminster that Italian soldiers were extremely adept in the art of 'drawing their swords, and cutting up a side street.'

FORMER LABOUR Chancellor Hugh Dalton was something of an enigma. He was highly intelligent, but according to a number of his contemporaries, he was also insincere, bombastic and flamboyant. His belligerence on occasions revealed a number of alarming prejudices. When the then Prime Minister Clement Attlee offered him a post at the Colonial Office, he is alleged to have replied: 'No bloody fear. They are a lot of syphilitic niggers.' And he described intellectuals in his own party as 'semi-crocks, diabetics and under-sized Semites.'

Just after the war, when he was Chancellor of the Exchequer, he was booming away to a journalist in the lobby and his voice could be heard in the chamber. This caused a Tory MP to comment: 'When Dalton whispers in the lobby, the seagulls take off at Battersea.'

He had not only a booming voice, but also a vicious

tongue. The following are some of his most acerbic oneliners on his colleagues and contemporaries:

On Oswald Mosley, when Mosley was a Labour MP: 'He stinks of money and insincerity!'

On Sir Charles Trevelyan, a fellow Labour MP, later Education Minister: 'He is almost incredibly stupid.'

On Clement Attlee: 'A small person with no personality.'

On Sir Stafford Cripps: 'He never knew a good point from a bad one. He is very vain and seems to think that only he knows what Socialism is.' And 'The man has the political judgement of a flea.'

His view of former Prime Minister Neville Chamberlain: 'The best thing that can be said of him is that, within the limits of his ignorance, he was rational, but I was appalled how narrow these limits were. It is clear that Hitler produced an enormous impression upon him. If Hitler had been a British nobleman and Chamberlain a British working man with an inferiority complex, the thing could not have been done better.'

When it became clear that Chamberlain's policy of appeasing Hitler had failed, Dalton was one of those who argued strongly that he must go. He remarked: 'The old man seems determined himself to stick to office – like a dirty old piece of chewing gum on the leg of a chair . . . he is incorrigibly limpet and is always trying new tricks to keep himself firm upon the rock.'

He hated his party colleague Emmanuel Shinwell who for a period was Minister of Fuel and Power: 'Shinbad the Tailor. He is by far the least attractive member of the government, always looking round for someone to whom to pass the blame. He will not face facts squarely. He is a coarse-grained shit and a low cur.'

His feelings were clearly reciprocated, Shinwell saying of him: 'Dalton's eyes have a habit of looking at you intently and conveying unfathomable depths of insincerity.'

Of Harry Truman, President of the United States, Dalton remarked: 'He is not an interesting man . . . completely platitudinous.'

When he was introduced to Sir Robert Menzies, the Prime Minister of Australia, they had a long and seemingly amiable chat, at the end of which Menzies said of the British Labour politician: 'You are a most extraordinary phenomenon – a Socialist with wit.' This prompted the barb from Dalton: 'You are a more extraordinary phenomenon still – a Conservative with intelligence.'

Although he admired the abilities of Labour left-winger Aneurin Bevan, he felt that the Welshman was an undisciplined talent who was too narcissitic: 'Megalomania and jealousy govern him – egoism and bitterness beyond all tolerable bounds.' He did not think much of Bevan's outlook on foreign affairs either: 'He was colour prejudiced – pro-black and anti-white.'

On the subject of Bevan, even Dalton's invective did not match that of one of his own backbenchers, Stanley Evans, who was Labour MP for Wednesbury. During a row over health charges, he accused Aneurin Bevan of 'leading an uneasy coalition of well-meaning emotionalists, rejects, frustrates, crackpots and fellow travellers, making Fred Karno's army look like a brigade of guards.'

Dalton showed his contempt for Labour MP James Griffiths of whom he said: 'A timid man who is frightened of his followers. He works on the principle "there go the people, I am their leader, I must follow them." '

On Labour MP Ian Mikardo: 'He was conceited, disloyal and over-rated.'

Of fellow Cabinet minister, and Labour Deputy Leader, Herbert Morrison: 'His sense of relative values is very weak and his outlook narrow. He is obstinate and ignorant.'

On Jim Callaghan: 'He is first class, though with no manners, and ruthless ambition.'

Commenting on Conservative Foreign Secretary, Selwyn Lloyd: 'A miserable third-rater if ever there was one.'

He was not a fan of Harold Wilson, saying of him in 1951: 'He is not a great success. He is a weak and conceited minister. He has no public face, but is frantically ambitious and desperately jealous of Hugh Gaitskell.'

Of Richard Crossman: 'He is hopeless – always adding some bright little variation of his own to other people's intrigues. He is one of the most unfaithful deceivers, with a coating of intellectual cheap glitter.'

On Sir Hartley Shawcross, former Labour MP and Government Minister: 'He ought to be called Sir Peacock. He is a mere time-server. He is insincere and vain, ego-soaked and impossible.'

When a Labour colleague – in discussions on the future leadership of the Labour Party – accused him of sitting on the fence, he retorted: 'I'd sooner sit on the fence than lie down in the shit on either side of it.' Although this silenced his friend, he did not have the last word on the subject. Fellow Labour MP Tony Crosland, overhearing the remark, interjected: 'That is a civilian's answer. In war, you have to lie in shit.'

When he believed strongly in something, his reply was not only tart, but frequently indelicate. When a Labour MP argued with him on the question of German rearmament, Dalton said that he had a conscience about the matter. His colleague did not believe him, going on to say that generally matters of conscience were such things as temperance and birth control. This led Dalton to explode: 'Do you tell me that I may have a conscience about beer bottles and French letters, but not about the life and death of my generation?'

In a similar vein, when Jim Callaghan said that a plan of Dalton's to try and encourage Aneurin Bevan to resign from the Labour party was 'too clever by half',

Dalton, who was irritated, replied: 'It is better to be too clever by half than too stupid by three-quarters.'

His ministerial career came to an abrupt end when his loose tongue caused him inadvertently to leak his financial proposals to journalists in advance of his Budget statement to the House of Commons and he was forced to resign.

Towards the end of his life, he found that he was becoming rather bored with the House of Commons and unflatteringly described his colleagues on the Labour benches as 'a row of ugly idiots'.

IN DUNDEE in 1908 the Independent candidate, G H Stuart, said of his opponent, 'He is a slippery gentleman – a fraudulent and dishonest politician and no friend to the workers.' The man about whom he said this – and who was safely elected – was Winston Spencer Churchill, now universally acknowledged as not just a great war leader but a master of the parliamentary insult.

It is well known that it is out of order to call an opponent a 'liar' in the House of Commons. Churchill was the first politician who managed to do so – within the rules of order – by referring to the remarks of an opponent as being a 'terminological inexactitude'.

As he came to power during the Second World War, it is not surprising that a number of Churchill's most memorable barbs were directed at Adolf Hitler. He said of the German leader: 'I always hate to compare Napoleon with Hitler, as it seems an insult to the great Emperor and warrior to connect him in anyway with a squalid caucus boss and butcher.' He later expressed a more colourful view. 'This bloodthirsty guttersnipe launches his mechanized armies upon new fields of slaughter, pillage and devastation.'

His comment on Germany was: 'They have proved

once again the truth of the saying that the Hun is always either at your throat or at your feet.'

On dictators generally he said, 'Dictators ride to and fro upon tigers which they dare not dismount.'

And his comments on Communist Russia were 'I cannot forecast to you the action of Russia. It is a riddle wrapped in a mystery inside an enigma.'

When Lord Inverchapel, Ambassador to the Soviet Union, asked what his policy towards Russia would be, Churchill replied: 'I don't mind kissing Stalin's bum, but I'm damned if I'll lick his arse.'

During the War, a senior naval officer complained that his service's role in the conflict was not in accordance with its great traditions. 'Well, Admiral, have you ever asked yourself what the traditions of the Royal Navy are?' Churchill responded. 'I will tell you in three words. Rum, sodomy and the lash.'

Speaking of France in the Second World War, he said. 'Although armed to the teeth, France is pacifist to the core.'

When it was announced that Tom Driberg, the Left-wing Labour MP, was to marry, quite a few eyebrows were raised. Driberg's homosexuality was well known at Westminster and when a photograph of the MP with his rather plain wife appeared in one of the daily papers, Churchill was moved to say: 'Oh well, buggers can't be choosers!' (On hearing the same news, another MP apparently remarked: 'Poor woman – she won't know which way to turn.')

Lambasting Labour leader Ramsay MacDonald: 'I remember when I was a child being taken to Barnum's circus . . . the exhibit which I most desired to see was one described as the "Boneless Wonder". My parents judged that the spectacle would be too revolting for my youthful eyes, and I have waited fifty years to see the Boneless Wonder sitting on the treasury bench.'

Of Ramsay MacDonald's oratory: 'He has, more

than any other man, the gift of compressing the largest number of words into the smallest amount of thought.'

On Lord Rosebery: 'He outlived his future by ten years and his past by more than twenty.'

He said of the Indian leader, Mahatma Gandhi: 'It is alarming and nauseating to see Mr Gandhi, a Middle Temple lawyer, now posing as a fakir of the East, striding half naked up the steps of the viceregal palace, whilst he is organizing and conducting a campaign of civil disobedience.' (Gandhi got his own back later, when he was asked in an interview what he thought about Western civilization. He is alleged to have replied, 'I think it would be a very good idea.')

Churchill was so adept at the parliamentary insult that he regularly used it as his main weapon during parliamentary question time. When a Labour MP named Wilfred Paling called Churchill 'a dirty dog', Churchill replied, 'If he is not careful, I will show him what a dirty dog does to a Paling!'

His description of the British Labour Party after the Second World War: 'They are not fit to manage a whelk stall.'

Commenting on Sir Redvers Buller, Commander-in-Chief of the Battle Forces, he said: 'He was a man of considerable scale. He plodded on from blunder to blunder and from one disaster to another, without losing either the regard of his country or the trust of his troops.'

On a poor speech by Lloyd George he said, 'Instead of making his violent speech without moving his moderate amendment, he would have been better to move his moderate amendment without making the violent speech.'

Replying to the MP William Kenyon-Slaney, who called him a traitor, he remarked: 'I have noticed when political controversy becomes excited, persons of choleric dispositions and limited intelligence are apt to become rude.'

In 1931, Churchill had survived the long process of leaving the Conservative Party to join the Liberals, only to seek to rejoin the Conservatives. He answered criticism with aplomb: 'Anyone can rat, but it takes a certain amount of ingenuity to re-rat.'

On George Wyndham MP: 'I like the martial and commanding air with which the right honourable gentleman treats facts; he stands no nonsense from them.'

His response to a woolly speech by Lord Charles Beresford: 'He can best be described as one of those orators who, before they get up, do not know what they are going to say; when they are speaking, do not know what they are saying; and when they have sat down, do not know what they have said.'

Commenting on Lord Kitchener: 'He had disapproved of me severely in my youth . . . it was a case of dislike before first sight.'

On socialist William Graham and his Budget proposals, Churchill said: 'He spoke without a note and almost without a point.'

His reaction to a risqué joke from a new MP: 'Young man, I predict you will go far . . . in the wrong direction.'

He was insulting but at the time accurate when he said of Japan: 'Their policy is to make hell while the sun shines.'

Just before the Second World War, in 1938 when he believed appeasement was a mistake, he said to Neville Chamberlain: 'You were given the choice between war and dishonour. You chose dishonour and you will have war.'

It is, as mentioned, unparliamentary for MPs to use the word 'liar' so the experienced parliamentarian needs either to think of an alternative or to be reasonably

"Winnie"

subtle in the way he phrases his criticism. Churchill said of another MP: 'Since the word "untruthfulness" has been used, no one has been a greater contributor than the honourable gentleman.' And, responding to a speech by the Labour MP, Aneurin Bevan, 'I should think it was hardly possible to state the opposite of the truth with more precision . . .'

When Aneurin Bevan became the Labour Minister of Health, he caused quite a furore by calling Conservatives 'lower than vermin', leading Churchill to say, 'Instead of bringing the balm of healing to the human heart, he has spoken of his fellow countrymen as "lower than vermin" . . . We speak of the Minister of Health, but ought we not to say, at least, the Minister of Disease?'

To Lord Winterton: 'He is a comparatively young Father of the House; he has many years of life before him. We still hope there may be years of useful life in this House, but unless in the future, his sagacity and knowledge of the House are found to be markedly superior to what he has exhibited today, I must warn him that he will run a very grave risk of falling into senility before he is overtaken by old age.'

After losing, by a landslide, the 1945 election, he was offered the Order of the Garter by George VI. He replied: 'I could not accept the Order of the Garter from my sovereign, when I have received the Order of the Boot from the people!' (He later changed his mind and was knighted in 1953.)

After the Labour landslide of 1945, it did not take him long to start insulting the new government. Of their foreign policy he said, 'Dreaming all night of giving away bits of the British Empire, and spending all day doing it.'

While he was listening to a boring speech in the House of Commons on statistics, he saw an elderly member with an antique ear trumpet leaning forward to hear the speech. He turned to the MP next to him and asked, 'Who is that idiot denying himself natural advantages?'

One of his Conservative colleagues once suggested that he would do better to stand on his dignity than to answer an attack levelled at him by an angry Labour MP. Churchill replied, 'I know of no case where a man added to his dignity by standing on it.'

When Sir John Foster was making a boring speech in the House, he noticed that Churchill had closed his eyes. Foster protested that Churchill was asleep and this brought the immediate response from Winston, 'I wish to God I were!'

When a Labour MP shouted at him, 'Must you fall asleep when I am speaking?' he replied, 'No, it is purely voluntary.'

Churchill's invective was often laced with sarcasm when he was attacking the Labour Prime Minister Clement Attlee. On one occasion he said, 'Mr Attlee, speaking of the achievements of his Labour government, said he was not satisfied with what had been done. His words were how can he clear up in six years the mess of centuries? "The mess of centuries!" This is what the Prime Minister considers Britain and her Empire represented when in 1945 we emerged honoured and respected from one end of the world to the other by friend and foe alike – after our most glorious victory for freedom. "The mess of centuries" – that is all we were. The remark reveals with painful clarity the Socialist point of view and sense of proportion. Nothing happened that was any good until they came into office. We may leave out the great struggles and achievements of the past – Magna Carta, the Bill of Rights, parliamentary institutions, constitutional monarchy, and the building of our Empire – all these were part of the "mess of centuries". Coming to more modern times, Gladstone and Disraeli must have been pygmies, Adam

Smith, John Bright and, in our lifetime, Balfour, Asquith and John Morley were no doubt all small-fry. But, at last, a giant and a Titan – Mr Attlee – has appeared to clear up the mess of centuries. Alas, he cries, he has had only six years to do it in, and now the Titan wants another term of office. The American declaration of independence said "All men are created equal", but the British Socialist party says "All men shall be kept equal".'

Although Churchill generally did not have much of an opinion of Attlee, during Attlee's spell as Prime Minister, he did seem to grow into the role and on one particular occasion made an excellent winding-up speech. A Conservative MP muttered to Winston that Attlee's speech was 'very good' and that he did not think Attlee could have made it eighteen months before. Churchill replied, 'Feed grubs royal jelly and they become queens.'

Soon after the war, when Churchill was Leader of the Opposition, he asked a number of questions which caused the Leader of the House, Herbert Morrison, to try to silence him with the remark: 'He really should recognize that another right honourable gentleman now presides over the Cabinet.' Without a moment's hesitation, Churchill rose and, with a flick of the hand towards Mr Attlee, said, 'I am indeed facing the fact – such as it is!'

Once he referred to one of his own party's back-benchers as 'that rising young stench'.

During a visit to Athens at the end of the Second World War, he was introduced to General Plastiras. Churchill is alleged to have muttered, 'Plasterass? Plasterass? I hope he hasn't got feet of clay too.'

On Field Marshal Montgomery: 'In defeat, indomitable; in victory, insufferable; in NATO, thank God, invisible.'

Lamenting the fact that after the Second World War

the Labour government continued rationing certain goods: 'Here you see clearly what is in their minds. The Socialist dream is no longer Utopia – but Queuetopia.'

And, disparaging Labour's early penchant for euphemisms, he said at a public rally, 'I hope you have all mastered the official Socialist jargon which they wish us to learn. You must not use the word "poor" – they are described as the "lower income group". When it comes to the question of freezing a workman's wages, they speak of "arresting increases in personal income" ' . . . 'they have a lovely one about houses and homes. They are in future to be called "accommodation units". I don't know how we are to sing our old song "Home Sweet Home"? "Accommodation unit, sweet accommodation unit – there's no place like our accommodation unit." I hope to live to see the British democracy spit all this rubbish from their lips.'

On Stanley Baldwin: 'Baldwin occasionally stumbles over the truth, but he always hastily picks himself up and hurries on as if nothing had happened.'

When someone in an audience threw a large cabbage in Churchill's direction during a speech, he said, 'I ask for the gentleman's ears – not his head.'

On being asked what was the difference between the Conservative and Labour outlook on policies for Britain, Churchill delivered a devastating and insulting rebuke to his Socialist opponents: 'The difference is the difference between the ladder and the queue. We are for the ladder. Let us all try our best to climb. They are for the queue. Let each wait in his place in the queue. The Socialists say if someone slips out of the queue they will have officials – and plenty of them – to put them back in it. When they say to us what happens if someone slips off the ladder, my reply is "We shall have a good net and the finest social ambulance service in the world".'

During one election campaign he was heckled by a

spotty-faced young man. Churchill finally lost his temper: 'I have always admired a manly man and I rejoice in a womanly woman – but I cannot abide a boily boy.'

Churchill's later view of the Liberal Party (of which he had once been a member): 'They are so few and so futile.'

Today there is continuing great talk of further European union in a number of areas. Churchill later favoured such an approach, but not for the armed forces. When he was asked in 1952 whether all national uniforms should be scrapped in favour of a European one, Churchill replied to his Secretary of Defence, Robert Lovett, 'No! That would be a sludgy amalgam.'

While Churchill was wearing his own uniform during a tour of duty, one of his epaulettes fell off. He remarked to his valet, Mr McGowan, 'It is a good job I personally fasten my braces.'

Later, when Field Marshal Sir William Slim suggested that a standard rifle for NATO forces could possibly be developed, Slim went on to say, 'I suppose we could experiment with a bastard rifle – partly American, partly British.' This drew the response from Churchill: 'Kindly moderate your language, Field Marshal. You may recall that I am partly British and partly American.'

What is endearing about Churchill is that very often, having attacked the opposition, he would turn the insults upon himself. Once, when he was asked if he was thrilled to realize that his speeches always brought a capacity audience, he responded, 'It is quite flattering, but whenever I feel this way, I always remember that if instead of making a political speech I was being hanged, the crowd would be twice as big.'

The presence of left-wing sympathizers in the Church is not new. In 1952 when the Dean of Canterbury, regarded by many as Communist, returned from China and Russia claiming that germ warfare had been used in Korea by the Americans, Churchill said, 'Free speech carries with it the evils of all the foolish, unpleasant and venomous things that are said – but on the whole, I would rather lump them than do away with it.'

When he was later questioned by a Labour MP called Lewis on the Korean War, and asked if he was aware of the 'deep concern felt by the people of Britain on the whole question of the Korean conflict', Churchill replied acidly, 'I am fully aware of the deep concern felt by the honourable member in many matters above his comprehension.'

On the British Labour Party's relationship with the United States of America he said, 'Any British government, Conservative or Socialist, will try hard to work with the United States. However, when the Socialists are in opposition, they cannot control their tail. It is hard enough for them to control their tail when they are in office.'

During the war, Churchill became dissatisfied with the content of BBC overseas broadcasts, feeling that they were too dispassionate. He wanted them to be more 'patriotic' in describing Britain's will to resist the Nazi threat, even if this meant taking liberties with the truth. He arranged a meeting with the Director-General of the BBC, Sir John Reith, an extremely tall man with a rather sour demeanour. Churchill tried, unsuccessfully, to persuade him to alter the tone of the overseas broadcasts but Reith insisted there should be no interference with the BBC's editorial integrity. (Where have I heard that before?) After the meeting, Churchill apparently said to one of his aides, 'Don't let that wuthering height darken my door again.'

When in opposition, the Conservative Shadow Cabinet met to consider what attitude it should take in respect of the Indian Independence Bill. The former Colonial Secretary, Oliver Stanley, who was the Conservative spokesman on India at the time, was not present at the beginning of the meeting and Churchill took advantage of his absence to express forcibly his own view – which was hostile to the bill. By the time Churchill had finished speaking, Stanley (who was a member of the Derby family) had arrived and was listening, somewhat stone-faced. As he concluded his remarks, Churchill turned to Stanley and said, 'Come on, Oliver. You agree we must oppose this bill.' To Churchill's surprise, Stanley shook his head and although Churchill urged him again to express his opposition to the bill, Stanley refused. Churchill then turned on him: 'You are like all the Derbys,' he spluttered. 'You arrive late on the battlefield and when you get there, you won't fight.'

During the harsh winter of 1947, the Minister of Fuel, Hugh Gaitskell, in an attempt to save on electricity consumption, urged the public to take fewer baths. During the course of his remarks, he said, 'I have never had a great many baths myself . . . it does not make a great deal of difference to your health if you have fewer.' He later said that this was a joke, but the damage was done. Winston Churchill rose in the Commons to comment: 'When Ministers of the Crown speak like this, they have no need to wonder why they are getting increasingly into bad odour. Mr Speaker, would you admit the word "lousy" as a parliamentary expression in referring to the government – purely as one of factual narrative.'

He said, retorting to someone who had made a speech of high-sounding clichés: 'It is wrong that these debates should proceed on a basis of guarded platitudes.'

After a poor speech by Ernest Bevin in which he rather sulked, Churchill referred to him as 'retiring behind a screen of inky fluid, like a cuttlefish, to some obscure hiding-place.' And on Welsh Labour MP Aneurin Bevan he said: 'Unless he improves, the most mischievous mouth in time of war will become the outstanding ministerial failure in time of peace.' This attack was so unexpected and bitter that it caught Bevan totally off guard. He crimsoned uncontrollably to his scalp before he managed to restrain himself.

When Churchill was barracked during one particular speech, he dismissed the murmurs with, 'The crackling of thorns beneath the pot does not disturb me.' This rather puzzled members of the opposition, until they realized that Churchill had found a perfectly parliamentary way of calling them fools through the means of a biblical quotation ('for as the crackling of the thorns under a pot, so is the laughter of fools' – Ecclesiastes VII, 6). And, to one Labour member who interrupted him without going through the formality of rising to his feet and asking him to 'give way', Churchill bellowed, 'The honourable gentleman is always interrupting – and this time he did not even bother to hop off his perch.'

Although he was usually ready to mix the insults with the opposition, on one particular day during the War – fed up with being heckled at question time by a tiny band of critics – Winston entered the House just in time for his questions and wearing a furious scowl. He sat down on the government front bench, folded his arms and continued to scowl. He answered his questions with a grim – and brief 'Yes, sir', or 'No, sir'. So flabbergasted were his critics, so worried that something had gone terribly wrong, that he was not asked a single supplementary question. When he left the chamber, he apparently roared with laughter and said, 'That shook 'em!'

Shortly after the General Strike, Churchill gave the Commons a demonstration of how he was able to defuse a row by a light-hearted insult. Some years earlier, he had been editor of the official government newspaper, the *British Gazette* – which not even his talents could prevent from being one of the dullest papers ever to be produced in Britain. During the debate, Churchill became the target of many Labour insults and tempers were running high.

He wound up the debate in a crescendo of fury and, as he approached his peroration he glared at Labour MPs opposite and shouted, 'And if you ever inflict on us another General Strike,' – and Labour MPs were barracking him all the time – 'I swear that we will inflict on you – ' He paused and scowled while the mutterings from the packed benches continued, and then leaned forward over the dispatch-box, and with every appearance of ferocity, shouted across the House, 'I swear that we will inflict on you – *another British Gazette.*' The scowl cleared from Churchill's face to be followed by a broad grin, and the whole House collapsed in helpless laughter.

In another debate the difference between Britain and some other countries was raised. He said, 'We have an educated democracy in this country, although' – and with a wave of his hand towards the Labour benches, he continued, 'you wouldn't think it to look at some of their temporary aberrations.'

Labour minister Emmanuel Shinwell had once returned from a European conference and was making a statement to the House about defence matters. His remarks contained just about every cliché known to officials, which led Churchill to respond: 'We are not much wiser – we will study what he has said and endeavour to see what meaning, if any, there is.' Mr Shinwell was not amused.

Many of his barbs were cutting, but it is chiefly the venom of his reported comments outside the chamber that have added weight to the Churchill legend since his death in 1965. It could be that one or two of the following remarks are apocryphal but the style is so definitely his, and the insults are so delicious, that I believe they do emanate from Winston Spencer Churchill, one of the greatest parliamentarians of all time. On Clement Attlee: 'He is a sheep in sheep's clothing.'

And on Clement Attlee's government: 'They are decided only to be undecided, resolved to be irresolute, adamant for drift, all-powerful for impotence.'

'Socialism is the philosophy of failure, the creed of ignorance and the gospel of envy.'

And on the Labour government: 'Government of the duds, by the duds and for the duds.'

On one of his colleagues: 'He has all the virtues I dislike and none of the vices I admire.'

On Joseph Chamberlain: 'Mr Chamberlain loves the working man – he loves to see him work.'

'An appeaser is one who feeds a crocodile, hoping it will eat him last.'

'The inherent vice of capitalism is the unequal sharing of blessings; the inherent virtue of Socialism is the equal sharing of miseries.'

'The difference between Balfour and Asquith is that Balfour is wicked and moral, Asquith is good and immoral.'

On seeing Sir Stafford Cripps walking through the smoking-room of the House of Commons: 'There but for the grace of God goes God.'

Of another's speech, 'Well, I thought it was very good. It must have been good, for it contained, so far as I know, all the platitudes known to the human race, with the possible exception of "prepare to meet thy God" and "Please adjust your dress before leaving".'

Churchill certainly did not spare the blushes of the fairer sex. When Labour MP Bessie Braddock accosted him with the remark: 'Winston, you are drunk, horribly drunk', he retorted, 'And Madam, you are ugly, terribly ugly, but in the morning I shall be sober.' And during an altercation with Lady Astor when she snapped at him, 'If I were your wife I'd put poison in your coffee',

Churchill silenced her with the response, 'If I were your husband, I'd drink it.'

In similar vein, on a trip to Paris, a colleague inquired why he had not brought his wife with him. Winston allegedly retorted, 'You don't take a sausage roll to a banquet.'

On democracy: 'Where there is a great deal of free speech, there is always a certain amount of foolish speech.'

On American politician John Foster Dulles: 'He is the only case I know of a bull who carries his own china with him.'

Although Churchill usually got the upper hand in insults, he did not always. Once Nye Bevan began a speech on the devaluation of the pound with the phrase that he welcomed the opportunity 'of pricking the bloated bladder of lies with the poniard of truth'. At this, Churchill objected and protested to the Speaker that surely the word 'lie' was out of order. Dismissing Churchill's objections, the Speaker responded blandly: 'Oh, I thought it was a quotation.'

On another occasion, after a meeting with Churchill, Field Marshal Montgomery (Monty) said, 'I have spent much of life fighting the Germans and fighting the politicians. It is much easier to fight the Germans.'

THE BRITISH House of Commons is often rightly referred to as 'the Mother of Parliaments' and if other assemblies in the West have deliberately copied our rules, standing orders and democratic customs, it can be no surprise that the members elected to these institutions spend a similar amount of time trading insults. One of the things I like about the United States is that, if anything, their vitriol is stronger!

One American politician has described US politics as

'the gentle art of getting votes from the poor, and campaign funds from the rich, by promises to protect each from the other'. In a similar vein, American journalist (and poet) Carl Sandburg wrote, 'A politician should have three hats. One for throwing in the ring, one for talking through and one for pulling rabbits out of, if elected.'

Here are some of my favourite barbs from across the Atlantic.

HAROLD L ICKES, who was Secretary of the Interior during the whole of Roosevelt's presidency and during the first year of Truman's, had quite a nice turn in insults. Of a senator from Louisiana he said: 'The trouble with Senator Long is that he is suffering from halitosis of the intellect – that's presuming he has an intellect.'

And Governor Talmadge of Georgia he dismissed as 'his chain-gang excellency'.

HERBERT HOOVER, the former US President, appeared to have something approaching contempt for those who praised 'the common man' in politics. He said, 'When we get sick, we want an uncommon doctor; if we have a construction job, we want an uncommon engineer; when we get into a war, we dreadfully want an uncommon general and an uncommon admiral. Only when we get into politics are we satisfied with the common man.'

And returning yet again to his theme: 'In my opinion, we are in danger of developing a cult of the common man, which means a cult of mediocrity.'

On the birth of his granddaughter, he remarked, 'Thank God, *she* doesn't have to be confirmed by the Senate.'

PRESIDENT WOODROW WILSON was refreshingly unpretentious. He had no time for those who are pompous, remarking, 'Some people come to Washington and grow with their jobs, but a lot of politicians come and all they do is swell up.'

He knew he was no oil painting and was fond of quoting a limerick that was grossly insulting to his own looks:

> As a beauty I am not a great star –
> There are others more handsome by far.
> But my face, I don't mind it
> Because I'm behind it –
> It's the folks in the front that I jar!

He also used to jokingly say of himself, 'I used to be a lawyer, but now I am a reformed character.'

Of course, he did not spend all his time in self-ridicule and frequently criticized severely those with whom he disagreed. Among his more pungent comments are the following:

On politician Chester Arthur: 'He is a non-entity with side whiskers.'

'A Conservative is a man who just sits and thinks – mostly just sits.'

Of a colleague: 'He is more apt to contribute heat, than light, to a discussion.'

And: 'All the extraordinary men I have ever known were chiefly only extraordinary in their own estimation.'

'The wisest thing to do with a fool is to encourage him to hire a hall and discourse to his fellow citizens. Nothing chills nonsense like exposure to the air.'

On Warren Harding: 'He had a bungalow mind.'

And Wilson's view of the first British Prime Minister was: 'William Pitt was a noble statesman; the Earl of Chatham was a noble ruin.'

Woodrow Wilson
smiles at one
of his own
witticisms

FORMER PRESIDENT Calvin Coolidge certainly was not noted for his wit. Indeed, he was not noted for his speeches, either, because he made a virtue of saying little. So terse was he that he drew this comment from an opponent: 'He is so silent that he is always worth listening to.'

When he was attending a banquet in Washington, a young woman who had heard that he was a man of few words said to him, 'I've made a bet with a friend that I can get you to say at least three words this evening.' The President replied, 'You lose.'

On one of the rare occasions when he spoke at some length, he raised more than a few eyebrows with the banal comment: 'If we allow high unemployment, there will be a lot of people out of work.' After a remark like that, he clearly could have been talking about himself when he later commented: 'Some people are suffering from lack of work, some from lack of water, many more from lack of wisdom.'

Possibly he might even have been serious when, at the end of his career, he said, 'I don't want to be President again, because there's no chance for advancement.'

THE LATE Henry Wallace had a healthy disregard for the sensitivities of the farming community – a trait most unusual among agriculture ministers. The former US Secretary for Agriculture had just said, 'This country should raise more wheat,' when a farmer shouted, 'What about hay?'

'I am speaking about food for mankind,' Wallace replied, 'but I'll get around to your case in a minute.'

For quick thinking, this ranks with the superb put-down by Tommy Douglas, former premier of the Canadian province of Saskatchewan. Calling him a pipsqueak, a heckler shouted, 'I could swallow you in one bite.' Without hesitation Douglas replied, 'And if you did, you'd have more brains in your belly than you have in your head.'

In his letters to his constituents, another American, Congressman John Steven McGroarty, was vitriolic. He once wrote: 'One of the countless drawbacks of being in Congress is that I am compelled to receive impertinent letters from a jackass like you, in which you say I promised to have the Sierra Madre mountains reforested and I have been in Congress two months and haven't done it. Will you please take two running jumps and go to hell.'

Fellow Yankee Senator Everett Dirksen would never have dreamt of using such language. His reason for always keeping his words 'soft, honeyed and warm' was, he said, 'Because as a politician I never know when I may be called upon to eat them.'

US PRESIDENT William Taft was decidedly corpulent and at a meeting Senator Chauncey Depew decided to crack an insulting joke about the President's size when introducing him to the gathered audience. During his opening remarks, Depew said, 'I hope, if it is a girl, President Taft will name it after his charming wife.' The President turned the insult back on Depew when he responded, 'If it is a girl, I shall, of course, name it for my lovely wife. And if it is a boy I shall claim the father's prerogative and name it Junior. But, if, as I suspect, it is only a bag of wind, I shall name it Chauncey Depew.'

UNLIKE COOLIDGE, President Theodore Roosevelt had a biting turn of phrase. He had no time for those whom he regarded as 'do-gooders', saying: 'Hardness of heart does nothing like as much harm as softness of head.'

He did not think much of the Upper House of Congress about which he gibed: 'When they call the roll in the Senate, the senators do not know whether to answer "present" or "not guilty".'

Among his other barbs are:

On the President of Columbia: 'A pithecanthropoid.'

Of his predecessor, President McKinley: 'He has about as much backbone as a chocolate éclair.'

On a university education: 'A man who has never gone to school may steal from a freight car – if he has a university education, he will probably steal the whole railroad.'

Of the American electorate: 'It may be that the voice of the people is the voice of God in fifty-one cases out of a hundred – but in the remaining forty-nine, it is quite as likely to be the voice of the devil, or, what is still worse, the voice of a fool.'

And even his own followers were not spared: 'The various admirable movements in which I have been engaged have always developed among their members a large lunatic fringe.'

THE DAUGHTER of President Teddy Roosevelt, Alice Roosevelt Longworth, as she became, had perhaps an even better line in insults than her father. She intensely disliked Senator Joe McCarthy and when he greeted her as 'Alice' she responded, 'Senator McCarthy, my gardener may call me Alice; all New York taxi drivers may call me Alice, the policemen on my corner may call me Alice, but *you* may call me Mrs Longworth.'

She enjoyed hearing abuse as well as dishing it out. At a party she made the delightful suggestion to a guest: 'If you can't say anything good about somebody, sit right down here beside me.' And when asked what she thought of President Coolidge, she responded that, 'He looked as if he had been weaned on a pickle.'

When the Republican Party picked New York governor Thomas Dewey to run against President Harry Truman in the 1948 election, she was heard to remark, 'How can the Republican Party nominate a man who looks like a bridegroom on a wedding cake?'

Even her own family did not go unscathed. Talking of Franklin Roosevelt, she said: 'Franklin is two-thirds mush and one-third Eleanor.'

FRENCH LEADER Charles de Gaulle did not think much of Franklin Roosevelt either. They first met in January 1943 and, it appears, took an instant dislike to each other. De Gaulle resented the fact that Roosevelt did most of the talking, and Roosevelt thought de Gaulle was too sure of his position as leader of the Free French forces. After the meeting, Roosevelt said to his Secretary of State, Cordell Hull, 'De Gaulle thinks that he is both Joan of Arc and Clemenceau.' Roosevelt's insult leaked, and soon appeared in the newspapers. When de Gaulle heard about the story, he was furious and exploded, 'I never again want to meet that President.'

At the time, not yet in government, de Gaulle complained, 'Since a politician never believes what he says, he is surprised when others believe him.'

FRANKLIN ROOSEVELT'S other gibes do not make him sound as 'mushy' as Mrs Longworth would have us believe. He gave his view of American radicals as 'men with both feet firmly planted in the air', but defined a liberal as 'A man who uses his legs and his hands at the behest of his head.' And he once silenced a crushing bore with the line: 'The ablest man I ever met is the man you think you are.'

However, at least one contemporary of his agreed

with Alice Longworth, saying that he was amusing but adding that he would 'not employ him as a geek in a common carnival.'

2
1945–1990: 'No Bloody Vision'

ANTHONY EDEN, Foreign Secretary under Winston Churchill and later Prime Minister, was a Conservative of the old school. In the House, his style was more that of a Foreign Office Diplomat than a political in-fighter. However, on at least one occasion, he knocked aside an opposition attack by the use of a low insult. He was being grilled by the Labour MP Tom Driberg, who, a few years earlier, had been taken to court for indecent assault. It was alleged at the trial that Driberg had made sexual advances to two men. Driberg was acquitted but details of the court case did not appear in the newspapers. The incident was suppressed by press magnate Lord Beaverbrook, for whom Driberg worked as columnist 'William Hickey.'

In the Commons, Driberg launched into a vicious attack on Eden during the course of which, he criticized the Tory Minister for 'flirtations with Kings.' Unusually – and rather out of character – Eden was stung to reply: 'I do not know how far the honourable member is an expert in flirtations, or in what kind of flirtations.' This stopped Driberg in his tracks who went white as a sheet whilst the House of Commons roared.

OLIVER STANLEY, the Conservative opposition spokesman on Finance just after the War, was regarded as an expert in the art of the insult. He was, however, a popular MP and there was great sadness – on both sides of the House – at his untimely death in 1950.

He frequently used the barbed comment to score points in debate. Once, during an all-night sitting of the

Finance Bill when the tax on admission as a barrister was being abolished, a long-winded back-bencher began to delve into the beginnings of the tax. He started at 1870, then moved to 1694 and then to the year of 1765. Stanley shouted: 'Will somebody tell me when he gets within a hundred years?'

When Clement Attlee was ill, Stanley voiced the sympathy of the House but added, 'None of us on the Conservative side really appreciates him as Prime Minister – until we begin to consider those who may possibly succeed him.'

On another occasion he devastated someone who interrupted his speech with the line: 'I wish the honourable gentleman's interruptions were as inaudible as they are unintelligible.'

Shortly after this, when Sir Stafford Cripps gave a tax concession on soda water, and said he expected to receive the thanks of the opposition, Stanley rose to his feet and to much amusement offered him 'diluted' thanks.

Cripps was not known for his sense of humour. During a debate on the Finance Bill he became annoyed by a violent attack from Stanley and told the House: 'Under the stress of speeches of that kind, I shall not be prepared to make accommodating offers to the House of Commons.' This caused Stanley to reply: 'The Chancellor of the Exchequer has given us to understand that future concessions are to be determined, not so much on the merits of each case, as on the flattery which the government receives. Not guns, but butter, has got to be the weapon of members in future.'

ONE OF the most effective Socialist parliamentarians during and just after the Second World War was the Welsh member Aneurin Bevan, who was blessed with a great gift of oratory.

He also had an extremely acerbic tongue and on more than one occasion he found himself in trouble for going 'over the top' in his use of invective. He caused uproar when he said in the 1940s: 'No amount of cajolery and no attempt at ethical and social seduction, can eradicate from my heart a deep burning hatred for the Tory Party . . . in so far as I am concerned, they are lower than vermin.'

He certainly enjoyed needling Conservative leader Winston Churchill, taunting him with, 'He never spares himself in conversation. He gives himself so generously that hardly anybody else is permitted to give anything in his presence.' At different times, he said of him: 'He is a man suffering from petrified adolescence.''The mediocrity of his thinking is concealed by the majesty of his language.' And: 'He refers to a defeat as a disaster, as though it came from God, but to a victory as though it came from himself.'

Of Florence Horsbrugh, Conservative Education Minister, he caused laughter on both sides of the House with his gibe that hers was a face that had 'sunk a thousand scholarships'.

He was one of the few Labour politicians who got the better of Harold Macmillan, of whom he said, 'He enjoys prophesying the imminent fall of the capitalist system and is prepared to play a part, any part, in its burial, except that of a mute.'

However, his Socialist colleagues could also feel the lash of his tongue. Upon a colleague complaining to Bevan that he was fed up with an unending round of luncheons and dinners to attend, Bevan snapped back, 'You're not an MP, you're a gastronomic pimp.' He seems to have been fond of this expletive. When he blew his top during a row with George Brown, he somewhat obscenely called him 'a pimp and a bastard.'

He did not appear to think much of his own party leader, Clement Attlee, and of the latter's style of speech said, 'He seems determined to make a trumpet sound like a tin whistle. He brings to the fierce struggle of politics the tepid enthusiasm of a lazy summer afternoon at a cricket match.'

Not many politicians have silenced Harold Wilson who, in his day, was the master of the Parliamentary put-down but Bevan did it when the two men were talking about Wilson's origins. At a party conference, Bevan had met Wilson's father who regaled him with stories of Labour election successes in the Manchester area in the early part of the century. When he met Harold, Nye said: 'I thought you said you were a Yorkshireman – but your father has been telling me all about Manchester. Where were you born, boy?' With a Yorkshireman's natural pride, Wilson replied, thinking of Sheffield's steel, 'Yorkshiremen are not born; they are forged.'

'Forged, were you?' riposted Nye. 'I always thought there was something counterfeit about you!'

He later said of Wilson: 'All bloody facts. No bloody vision.'

R A BUTLER, known to friend and foe alike as 'Rab', shot out a double-edged insult when he was once asked by Labour MP Marcus Lipton whether the then Prime Minister, Harold Macmillan, was not trying, on the question of doctors' pay, to tiptoe out of an impossible situation. 'He is not,' replied Rab, and added that 'In any case, the Prime Minister is not nearly so flat-footed as Colonel Lipton.'

When he was asked about whether the Festival of Britain funfair in Battersea Park should be opened on a Sunday, it was put to him by a back-bench MP that he had received 'thousands of postcards on the subject'. This led Rab to silence him with the response that

'Legislation by reflection is surely preferable to legislation by postcard.'

HAROLD MACMILLAN was a skilful politician and a successful Prime Minister until the Profumo scandal hit his administration when, suffering a breakdown in health, he decided to resign. Some years earlier, when asked by a journalist a particularly inane question about what objectives he wished the public to aspire to, he retorted, 'If people want a sense of purpose, they should get it from the archbishop. They should certainly not get it from their politicians.'

Commenting on a colleague: 'He is forever poised between a cliché and an indiscretion.'

During the period of the Cold War, Macmillan had to address the Security Council of the United Nations. Sitting near to him was the Russian leader, Nikita Khrushchev. During his speech, Macmillan made a number of points with which Khrushchev disagreed strongly. In the end, Khrushchev became so enraged with what was said that he took off one of his shoes and banged the heel on the table in protest. Displaying his typically British style and aplomb, and not appearing in the least perturbed by Khrushchev's outrageous insult, Macmillan asked urbanely, 'I wonder if I could have a translation?' He did show signs of irritation in the early 1960s when the leader of the Labour Party, Harold Wilson, claimed to the Press that when he was a boy, his family were too poor to afford to buy him any boots. Macmillan snapped, 'If Harold Wilson ever went to school without any boots, it was merely because he was too big for them.'

KHRUSHCHEV DID not always communicate through his footwear and during his career he made some gibes which the Tory premier would probably have approved, including 'Politicians are the same all over. They promise to build a bridge even when there is no river.'

And a comment that could have come straight from Mac himself: 'If you live among wolves, you have to act like a wolf.'

More in character was his remark 'If someone hits me on the left cheek, I would not turn my own. I would hit him on the right cheek – and so hard that it would knock his head off.'

THE COLOURFUL Tory back-bencher Sir Gerald Nabarro was a delightful eccentric who in his day frequently delivered broad and obvious insults against MPs of all parties, including his own.

No one who met him could be in any doubt that he was an expert in the art of Parliamentary invective. He frequently referred to opponents' speeches as 'drivelling rot' and on one occasion he said of a speech by Shirley Summerskill: 'I suppose that it would be a parliamentary courtesy for me to congratulate the right honourable lady on her maiden speech as Secretary of State for Employment. I do so only as a parliamentary courtesy. The content of her speech was unimpressive, unconvincing, flatulent and flabby.'

He was an expert on the subject of purchase tax and he launched a long, and ultimately successful, campaign for its abolition. In December 1956, he said of a speech by his own Chancellor of the Exchequer, Harold Macmillan: 'I was captivated by the Chancellor's reply on the fourth of December, and I have been poring over it ever since. I have been trying to determine exactly what he meant.'

At the time of the Profumo affair, during Macmillan's premiership, Nabarro was even more vitriolic. 'Mr Macmillan must shuffle his pack. He must put new men into office and get rid of the deadwood and rotten ministers. He must sack the dunderheads.'

Commenting on Macmillan's successor, Sir Alec Douglas-Home, he said: 'He created the impression of being rather dated, rather fuddy-duddy, rather aristocratic, indifferent in health and altogether too well-mannered and gentle for politics in the age of Harold Wilson.'

Nabarro's main fault was that he could not resist the limelight, and, despite frequent advice from his colleagues not to comment about what was happening in his own party, he was regularly to be seen or heard, on one chat show or another, blasting off about someone in the news. Asked again about the new Tory leader, Sir Alec Douglas-Home, he added to his earlier remarks: 'Sir Alec's image is dull, stodgy and dated. Those silly bags behind a shot-gun, blowing off on grouse moors and counting with matchsticks, are all reminiscent of a past age and make poor showing for the Tories.'

Although he sometimes expressed admiration for the qualities of the Labour premier, Nabarro also said, 'When it comes to naked party politics, no Prime Minister has ever made such an idiot of himself by flagrantly broken promises as Mr Harold Wilson.'

Long before Enoch Powell was sacked from the Shadow Cabinet by Edward Heath, he said of the former: 'He has an assortment of largely disingenuous and gratuitously bizarre opinions.' He did not think much of Heath either, commenting that 'his style of oratory remains pedantic, matter-of-fact, and highly economic in words, passion and beauty.' When Heath became Conservative Party leader it was initially thought that he would be a good match for Harold Wilson. Nabarro, however, was not convinced, telling the Press: 'Heath is prosaic, unexciting and unpersonable.'

During a debate, he dismissed comments by Michael

Foot, with the barb: 'His knowledge of industry could be accommodated on the back of a fourpenny stamp.' And in the early 1970s, airing his views on the decline of the Liberal Party, he observed that it was 'the shadow of a splinter.'

When he believed in an issue, he did not care whom he insulted. He told his own electors that he would campaign for higher pay for MPs whatever their view, adding: 'Hypocrisy, snobbery, self-indulgence and the under-payment of Members of Parliament are hall-marks of the British public and I doubt whether they will ever change.'

Disgusted with what he regarded as a banal speech by Labour MP Albert Murray, he called him a 'mere flatulent lightweight.'

Labour MP Robert Sheldon did not impress him either: 'His speech was characteristic first for its longevity and secondly, for its muddleheadedness. He is the leader of that back-bench school of thought which has groped for office in Labour governments, but which has never achieved it.'

It has been said that Sir Gerald was self-centred, egotistical and at times, impossible. Indeed he was. But he was never dull, and he livened up many a dreary debate with his entertaining banter and colourful abuse. Of himself, just before his death in 1973, he said, 'Half the nation swears by me, the other half at me.'

THE LATE Lord Mancroft was well known for his sense of humour. He it was who subtly insulted his fellow countrymen with his description of cricket: 'A game which the English, not being a spiritual people, have invented to give themselves some conception of eternity.'

On equality, Mancroft remarked, 'All men are born equal, but quite a few get over it.'

IF JUDGED by his period in office, a total of eight years, Harold Wilson must be regarded as the most successful Labour Party leader of all time. I do not pass comment on his achievements or his mistakes, as that is not the purpose of this book. What is important here is that throughout his parliamentary career he has shown that he had a ready, willing and sometimes inspired line in insults. Also, as with a number of Prime Ministers both before and since, he has shown himself willing – sometimes eager – to take a verbal swipe at members of his own party, including some former members of his Cabinet.

After the 1983 election, when asked his view about the decision taken by the Labour Party in future to choose its leader by an electoral college, he indicated that he disagreed with the proposal. He went on to explain that the Queen might need a Prime Minister immediately after an election, particularly in a time of crisis, and that the monarch should not have to wait for the Labour Party to choose its own leader. But then, showing a flash of his old self, he told the journalist that he was 'not the right man to ask' because he did not know much about such matters. He went on to say that he had 'very little experience of the Labour Party not being in power' thus taking a hard swipe at subsequent leaders of his own party.

During the War, before he entered politics, Wilson had the chance to work with William Beveridge on a number of projects. Of Beveridge he has said: 'He was a devil to work for. He was absolutely certain that he was right about everything but he was a political innocent. As a practical administrator he was a disaster because of his arrogance and rudeness and his total inability to delegate.'

He also did not have much of an opinion of his former colleague Herbert Morrison. When, after the 1950 election, the Labour Party held a private inquest into its disastrous election result, Wilson commented: 'The inquest was masterminded by Morrison. The Press were, of course, not present but Herbert Morrison was, so they were saved the journey.'

His view of Harold Laski was that he was: 'learned, but lacking in plain common sense.'

And his view of Ernest Bevin, one of his colleagues in the Attlee government: 'Ernie Bevin had a congenital attitude veering from deep suspicion to ill-concealed hatred of the Russians.'

He has been caustic when giving his view of his immediate predecessor as Labour leader, Hugh Gaitskell, remarking: 'Once he came to a decision, any colleague taking a different line from his was regarded not only as an apostate but as a trouble-maker or simply a person lacking in brains. As party leader, he was far too didactic in his speeches and public appearances, adopting more the manner of an Oxford don explaining economic theory than seeking to identify himself in homely terms with the electorate. He had no knowledge of how ordinary people thought.' And he dismissed former Labour Chancellor Hugh Dalton with the line: 'Apart from his loud voice, he had little to commend him.'

Commenting on Tom O'Brien, the former leader of the National Association of Cine Employees, Wilson has been positively bitchy: 'He suffered more than any other trade union leader from the malady known as enuresis – being a propensity for leaking when Pressmen are about.'

If Wilson did not have much respect for many of his Labour colleagues, he was biting in his criticism of Tory premier Anthony Eden. Commenting on Eden's performance as Prime Minister he said, 'On foreign affairs he thought that he knew where he was. But a Prime Minister has to deal with economic affairs, home affairs, unemployment and constituency problems

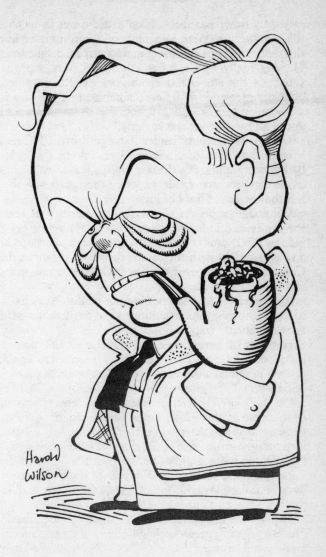

Harold
Wilson

raised by other members. Eden just did not fit in with this routine. At Prime Minister's question time, he had the replies written out for him and just read them out. He was really rather a pathetic figure, very sophisticated, on the whole too much Foreign Office trained, perfectly nice and hardly ever capable of saying boo to a goose. When he did say boo, he chose the wrong goose and said it far too roughly.'

On his own deputy leader, George Brown: 'When I brought him into government, I was taking a risk. He had erratic habits. His drink problem was always with us. It was not that he drank more than anybody else, but that he could not hold it.'

Commenting on the Conservative Secretary of State for Trade and Industry, John Davies: 'He was a good manager but was a fish out of water in Parliament and was baited with the same relish by Labour as the Conservatives had used on Frank Cousins a few years earlier.'

'Conservative Ministers of Labour tend to be as uninformed on trade union realities as some Labour MPs are on financial institutions.'

His view of Tony Benn: 'He immatures with age.'

And on Roy (now Lord) Jenkins: 'He tended to knock off at seven o'clock . . .' a socialite rather than a Socialist.'

On former MP Willie Hamilton: 'He refers to hangers-on of the Royal Family but I doubt whether there is anyone better rewarded, or who is a greater beneficiary, from the existence of the monarchy, through his writings, than he.'

He is alleged to have said of one of his own party's back-benchers, David Winnick: 'He's the silliest man in the House.'

His view of the journalists who work for the tabloid Press is, perhaps, predictable: 'What do you expect from a pig, but a grunt?'

And on P G Wodehouse: 'He had a naïve insistence on visiting Hitler's Berlin and broadcasting unpatriotic claptrap on radio during the war.'

On Denis Healey: 'He is a strange person. His method of thinking is that he is absolutely certain that he is right and everybody else is wrong – and not merely wrong through not knowing the proper answers, but wrong through malice.'

On two of colleagues: 'Herbert Bowden and Ted Short are excellent bureaucrats, but they have no political nous at all.'

During a debate in the House, Wilson was wickedly insulting during an attack on the Conservative Minister, Duncan Sandys, and the Blue Streak defence missile project, which he regarded as mistaken. Wilson gibed: 'We all know why Blue Streak was kept on although it was an obvious failure. It was to save the Minister's face. We are, in fact, looking at the most expensive face in history. Helen of Troy's face, it is true, may only have launched a thousand ships, but at least they were operational.'

Later, when he was addressing a meeting in Glasgow, a young man persistently interrupted his speech with shouts of 'groundnuts'.* Wilson retorted: 'There's an ageing Young Conservative . . . his only contribution to the Blue Streak argument is to shout "groundnuts" . . . where have you been, Rip Van Winkle?'

IAIN MACLEOD was a brilliant debator whose untimely death in 1970 robbed the Conservative Party

---

* In 1947, the Labour Minister of Food pursued a scheme for clearing more than 3 million acres in East Africa to produce 600,000 tonnes of groundnuts by 1951, thereby saving £10m from Britain's food bill. The project turned into a financial disaster and £37m of public money was lost. The policy was abandoned in 1950.

of one of their heavy-weight performers. Although he had a remarkable talent for rousing a party audience, it was his devastating use of ridicule and mockery in debate for which he will be remembered by friend and foe alike.

In Opposition, he hit the mark when replying to Roy Jenkins, the Labour Chancellor of the Exchequer. Looking across at him, he sneered: 'The contempt he feels for my right honourable friends on this side of the House is exceeded only by the disdain he feels for his own right honourable friends on his side of the House.'

During a discussion, he was asked by fellow Conservative MP Enoch Powell whether he would give his support in being against statutory wage control. MacLeod, who agreed up to a point, took a swipe at what he regarded as Powell's somewhat extreme stance on the issue. He confirmed his general support and added: 'I am a fellow traveller, but I prefer to get out one or two stops before the train crashes into the buffers at the terminus.' He was later to say of Powell: 'He suffers from an excess of logic.'

In 1952, MacLeod made a devastating attack on Aneurin Bevan, who had been Minister of Health in the outgoing Labour government and was regarded by many as the architect of the National Health Service. The debate was on a Bill which sought to impose prescription and dental charges which the Labour Government had agreed to when in office but had not implemented. MacLeod started: 'I want to deal closely and with relish with the vulgar, crude and intemperate speech to which the House of Commons has just listened.' He then launched into a devastating attack on Bevan, commenting: 'A debate on the National Health Service without the Right Honourable Gentleman would be like putting on *Hamlet* with no one in the part of the first grave-digger.' He went on, sarcastically, to say 'the Right Honourable Gentleman went down about a month ago to explain his conduct in the House to his constituents – something which I gather is in the nature of an annual event . . . ' MacLeod then quoted Bevan as having given an assurance that in respect of Health Service cuts, he would not be restrained by any previous commitments made by anyone. He went on to comment that no one could complain of Bevan's enthusiasm, since he had made it quite plain that he was 'not going to be restrained, even by the commitments he had made himself'. This attack was unexpected but extremely effective. Churchill, then Prime Minister, was so impressed, he promoted MacLeod shortly after-wards.

During his period as Minister of Labour, he made mincemeat of a Labour motion deploring a rise in unemployment which contained inaccurate figures. Taking a swipe at the Opposition spokesman, Douglas Jay, MacLeod commented: 'I have no doubt that he will improve. The first seven years in opposition are always the most difficult. There is no point in his getting cross with me. I did not put this motion on the Order Paper – the opposition did and I cannot help it if every time the Labour Party are asked to name their weapons they pick boomerangs.'

And his comments on Labour Chancellor Hugh Gait-skell: 'He is Mr Rising Price himself.'

After being attacked in the Commons by Harold Wilson, MacLeod retorted: 'The speech which he (Wilson) has just delivered was, as always, witty, cogent and polished . . . and polished . . . and polished. He paid me the great compliment of saying that to this debate I had brought a fresh mind. I wish that he would bring a fresh speech.' He went on to say of the Labour leader: 'J F Kennedy has described himself as an idealist without illusions. Harold Wilson is an illusionist with-out ideals. Double-talk is his mother tongue. He is a man whose vision is limited to tomorrow's headlines.'

He continued in the same crushing form: 'This country has only had three Socialist Prime Ministers and each one of them has devalued the pound. This is no coincidence except the coincidence of incompetence.'

On Jim Callaghan: 'He suffers from what you may regard as a fatal defect in a Chancellor. He is always wrong.'

Shortly after becoming Chancellor of the Exchequer himself, in 1970, he responded to a suggestion by Wilson that the Tory Government should pay heed to the need to keep election promises. MacLeod retorted: 'Look who is talking. The walking waste-paper basket himself, filled with lightly given promises and pledges.'

During his career, MacLeod received a back-handed compliment from Labour MP Michael Foot, who said of him: 'Don't under-rate Mr Iain MacLeod. He is much the most intelligent Member of the Stupid Party.'

LORD HAILSHAM is, I believe, the longest-serving living politician in Britain today and the only surviving member of Winston Churchill's administration. He has served under every Conservative Prime Minister since (apart from John Major), only retiring as Lord Chancellor in 1987. He was, and is, a lively and colourful speaker.

One of his most effective and striking (literally) attacks was on Harold Wilson during the 1966 General Election. Quintin Hogg, as he then was, was addressing an open-air rally when a Labour supporter, standing near to the platform, raised a large placard on which was pasted a poster showing the head and shoulders of Wilson with the words 'You Know Labour Government Works' printed underneath. Hogg immediately turned the incident to his own advantage by asking the crowd to look at the poster – 'the one with the ugly face.' He then launched into a violent attack on the placard with his walking stick. The young Socialist was helpless. He was anchored to his place by the crowd and could not move. He was obliged to stand there, struggling to hold on to poster and board, while a senior member of the Shadow Cabinet smashed it to smithereens. The whole incident was recorded by the television cameras present and even today, some twenty-five years later, it is still a highly amusing, but effective, piece of political theatre.

A Hailsham speech is always entertaining and usually contains an insult or two. Among his most memorable are the following:

'Much . . . of a Commons debate is often a dreary mass of ill-informed and almost unreadable verbiage.'

On the Labour government's Social Contract: 'As a means of containing inflation or securing industrial peace, it has done neither. You might as well try to control a rutting elephant with a pea-shooter.'

On religion: 'The man who puts politics first is not fit to be called a civilized being, let alone a Christian.'

And in a slightly more typical vein: 'If the British public falls for the programme of the Labour Party, I say it will be stark raving bonkers.'

On the tendency of some Labour supporters to pacifism: 'They have a curious belief that bullies are cowards. In my experience, this is not the case when they are faced with a manifestly weaker opponent.'

'When I first entered the House of Commons, I was still young, inexperienced and prone to arrogance.'

Of former MP George Griffiths: 'He was a Labour MP of the flat-capped breed.'

On Clement Attlee: 'A rather mean-minded, waspish man.'

Of Lord Birkenhead (F E Smith), whom he met when the former Lord Chancellor visited Oxford: 'He had an arrogant gift of crushing repartee.'

His view of Cabinet colleague, R A Butler: 'I never numbered candour amongst his virtues . . . he had not the stuff within him of which Prime Ministers are made. Politics may well include the art of the possible, but weakness on matters of principle, coupled with an inability to admit that you are wrong, limits the area of what is possible.'

And on Rab Butler's decision to serve under Alec Douglas-Home rather than challenge him for the leadership, he commented: 'Ferdinand the Bull had preferred to sniff the flowers rather than take what would have been his if he had wished it.'

On a former MP, Harry Legge-Bourke: 'A narrow-minded but honourable patriot.'

On Labour's plans to cut the powers of the House of Lords: 'The Parliament Act of 1949 was one of the more absurd and useless statutes passed by the Attlee government and characteristic, I believe, of the muddled and unprincipled way in which Herbert Morrison managed the affairs of the Labour Party.'

On the difference between the House of Commons and the House of Lords: 'Television has greatly enhanced the prestige and influence of the House of Lords, which presents an intelligent and informed contrast to the monkey-house noises emanating from Prime Minister's question time in the Commons.'

'Socialism may be an excellent way of sharing misery, but it is not a good way of creating abundance.'

With Lord Hailsham, one feels that the vivid turn of phrase is always just beneath the surface, waiting to burst out at moments of irritation. In the early 1950s, the Dean of Canterbury provoked the crack, 'He is a clown in gaiters'; a decade or so later Maltese premier Dom Mintoff elicited the observation that he was a 'somewhat hysterical figure', while the one-time MP and Air Minister Nigel Birch was described as 'nervy, and prone to fits of threatening resignation'.

On the occasion when Michael Heseltine stormed out of a Cabinet meeting and resigned from the government,

Hailsham has said: 'The only moral I can draw from histrionic performances of this nature is that they should not normally happen . . . the dignity of Cabinet government is hardly enhanced by dramatic charades or displays of personal passion.'

And his view of the late Dick Crossman: 'Utterly unscrupulous. But he was never able to develop a single coherent political theme. Moral principle was not his strong suit.'

Hailsham met Russian leader Nikita Khrushchev on more than one occasion and has given a vivid cameo of the man with his remarks: 'His coarseness of language and anecdote absolutely beggared description. His changes of mood between the aggressively ferocious and comradely genial never ceased to astonish me. He was a rhinoceros of a man with veins standing out on his forehead.'

Of Prime Minister Margaret Thatcher: 'You've got to put her in the same category as Bloody Mary, Queen Elizabeth I, Queen Anne, and Queen Victoria. However, she reminds me most of Queen Elizabeth I out of those four. Her handling of men is not dissimilar. I mean, if you had been a courtier of Queen Elizabeth I, you would never have known quite whether you were going to get the treatment of an admired friend, or a poke in the eye with an umbrella.'

Commenting on his early diet: 'Not for me the heresies of healthy eating favoured by Edwina Currie, or the hypochondriacal fears of cholesterol.'

Despite visiting Blackpool virtually every other year, on the occasion of the Conservative Party Conference, he clearly has no love of the place, describing the resort thus: 'It may be famous for fresh air and fun, but apart from the tower and the funfair, it is endowed by nature with a sea which is rough and cold and somewhat redolent of human effluent.'

Even at the end of his ministerial career, his wicked

sense of humour – and penchant for insults – had not deserted him. During a rather tedious speech by the Bishop of Durham, a Labour peer entered the chamber, perusing some papers, when he heard a loud voice say: 'What a load of bollocks.' Astonished, he looked up at the public gallery, expecting to see a demonstrator being led away – but all was calm. It was only as he approached his seat that he realized the comments had come from the occupant of the Woolsack – Lord Hail-sham.

WILSON'S DEPUTY Prime Minister, as I have mentioned, was George Brown, an able but extremely unpredictable character, particularly when he had had a drink. During the 1964–66 Labour government, when the Party was unpopular in the polls, senior Cabinet ministers had a discussion to decide what they could do to reverse the trend. Brown listened to a number of high-minded speeches and – then entirely typically – vigorously argued that the Labour Party had been 'guilty of too much morality and not enough politics.'

When some colleagues were talking over the merits of the Sexual Offences Bill, which relaxed the law on homosexuality, George Brown, who was listening, exploded. He became extremely aggressive and insulting of homosexuals, saying, among other things, 'Society ought to have higher standards; if this Bill gets through we will have a totally disorganized, indecent and unpleasant society. We've gone too far on sex already.' Then, to the surprise and astonishment of those present, he added: 'I don't regard any sex as pleasant. It's pretty undignified and I've always thought so.' His last remarks raised a few eyebrows, particularly as Brown frequently went through the far more public indignity of being hopelessly drunk.

During this period *The Times* found some support

on the Labour benches for its remark: 'George Brown drunk is a better man than the Prime Minister sober.'

ONE OF the most successful women in Labour governments has been Barbara Castle. She held the offices of Minister of Overseas Development, Minister of Transport, the Secretary of State for Employment and Productivity, all under the premiership of Harold Wilson.

However, during her period of office, she was also one of the most unpopular ministers ever, due principally to the Road Safety Act of 1967, which, as Transport Minister, she piloted through the Commons. This measure introduced the breathalyzer to Britain and so incensed the beer-swilling motorist (at that time probably in the majority) that almost overnight graffiti appeared on many road bridges, sometimes written in an unsteady hand, proclaiming: 'BAN THE BAG'. No one at the time was in any doubt about who the bag was.

She was sacked by Jim Callaghan when he took over leadership of the Labour Party in 1976.

She had – and has – a sharp tongue and frequently used it against her own colleagues. Of Wilson's first Cabinet she said: 'It was the most talkative Cabinet in political history.'

And on former Cabinet minister Tony Crosland: 'He had a brilliant academic mind and made a big impact with his book, *The Future of Socialism*, but he failed to carry analysis into action.'

Of her own boss she remarked: 'Harold Wilson seems to have a streak of vulgarity which is also part of his strength.'

Many Conservatives would these days probably agree with her gibe made during the 1960s that Ted Heath was 'stiff and uncharismatic'.

Over the years, she had made a number of barbed

Barbara Castle.

Diary notes

comments of which the following are the most memorable:

On George Brown: 'He really was a tragic figure: so much ability linked to so much instability.'

On former Labour politician Ray Gunter: 'He spat out his views with his typical philistine venom.'

On Jim Callaghan (following his move from the office of Chancellor of the Exchequer): 'He is obviously smarting all the time under the implication that he failed as Chancellor and is retrospectively justifying everything he did.'

On Roy Hattersley in 1969: 'I don't think he is a particularly nice man.'

ON BEING replaced by John Davies and returning to the Tory back-benches, an unhappy Reginald Maudling offered the sarcastic explanation: 'There comes a time in every man's life when he must make way for an older man.'

MICHAEL FOOT, veteran MP and former leader of the Labour Party, does not think much of our National Anthem. According to him: 'The tune is appalling and the words are banal.'

Of the Tories, he once remarked: 'There never was a more bloody-minded set of thugs than the British ruling class.'

However, although an effective orator, many view his period as Labour leader as an absolute disaster. At the time of the 1983 General Election, when Labour's fortunes hit rock bottom, he was described as 'a sort of walking obituary for the Labour Party'.

Usually Norman Tebbit is on the giving end of insults, but on one particularly memorable occasion, he was the victim. Michael Foot described him as 'a semi house-trained polecat.' He has subsequently modified his view, saying of Tebbit: 'He is the most stupendously offensive man in the House.'

And recently – after a Cabinet minister admitted he was too busy to read any books, 'Men of power have no time to read; yet the men who do not read are unfit for power.'

ON ANOTHER occasion Foot, commenting on the first 100 days of John Major's premiership, said: 'Napoleon in his 100 days recaptured Paris without a battle. John Major in his 100 days buried Thatcherism without a tear. Thereafter they were both destroyed for their previous misdeeds.'

TORY PRIME MINISTER Edward Heath struck a chord with many when he commented on the high fees of directors of Lonrho as 'the unpleasant and unacceptable face of capitalism'.

And expressing his views on his political colleagues he has said, 'No one knows better than a former chief whip the limitations of the human mind and the human spirit.'

However, since he lost the Tory leadership, he has alienated many members of the Conservative Party by his enduring hostility to his immediate successor and his lack of support for her policies. Tory MP George Gardiner probably spoke for many Conservatives when he said: 'Receiving support from Ted Heath in a by-election is like being measured by an undertaker.'

FORMER LABOUR front-bencher Denis Healey has earned the nickname of the 'Old Bruiser'. He can be a brilliant knock-about performer, usually being the one doing all the knocking. When he is on form he has a devastating turn of invective. Many Conservative politicians were amazed, but for electoral reasons pleased, that he failed to become Labour Party leader before the 1983 election. His low swipe at the Deputy Prime Minister a few years back – 'being attacked by Sir Geoffrey Howe is like being savaged by a dead sheep' – is vintage Healey, although it was Sir Geoffrey who had the last 'bite', as it were. When Healey retired from Labour's front bench some time after his broadside had been delivered, it was Howe who resurrected the incident with the rejoinder that Healey's final tributes were akin to being 'cherished by a dead savage'.

Mr Healey has also shown that he is not averse to insulting royalty. On being told by Prince Charles that his was a lonely life, Healey reputedly replied, 'Well you shouldn't have taken the job then, should you?'

Healey is still regarded as one of the Labour Party's most effective performers. Largely due to his knockabout style with insults. His main speciality appears to be insulting former Prime Minister Margaret Thatcher, usually in highly florid and colourful language.

He once accused her of behaving like 'a superannuated Sumo wrestler'. And of her policies, he snapped, 'She adds the diplomacy of Alf Garnett to the economics of Arthur Daley.'

Commenting on Mrs Thatcher in 1987: 'When Mr Reagan tells Mrs Thatcher to jump, her only reply is "how high?" '

And: 'I often compare Margaret Thatcher with Florence Nightingale. She stalks through the wards of our hospitals as a lady with a lamp – unfortunately, it is a blowlamp.'

He once even compared Mrs Thatcher to President Castro, calling her 'the Castro of the Western world – an embarrassment to all her friends'. He went on to add: 'All she lacks is the beard.'

'The Prime Minister says that she has given the French President a piece of her mind – this is not a gift I would receive with alacrity.'

And more: 'She seems bent on undermining most of the institutions which provide social tissue for our parliamentary democracy . . . she seems to have lost that instinct for the popular mood which marked her first two terms.'

And yet again: 'She is not just a female Franco, but a Pétain in petticoats.'

In 1983, after the Falklands victory, he said of her: 'She glories in slaughter.' (This caused such an outcry that he later modified the criticism to 'she glories in conflict'.)

Admitting, with some regret, that he failed in his main ambition to become leader of the Labour Party: 'It's no good sulking in your tent like Ted Heath. That's really appalling.' He went on to take a further swipe at Heath with the barb: 'There is an element of stony rigidity in his make-up which tends to petrify his whole personality in a crisis.'

Of Mrs Thatcher's Cabinet, Healey has said: 'The only loyal supporter is Kenneth Baker. He reminds me of Nasser's chief of staff who said his position was one hundred per cent loyalty – until the time for treachery arrives.'

Of former Labour colleague, David Owen: 'An odd fellow . . . he is incapable of working in a team. He's like the upas tree – poisons the ground for miles around.' And commenting on Owen's period as Labour's Foreign Secretary: 'He began to mask his insecurity with an arrogance which was found offensive.'

Healey's robust invective sometimes – as you would expect – gets him into hot water, like the time when he said of his own party leader: 'Neil Kinnock is politically intelligent, has character and courage . . . but has never been made a minister, lacks experience, and people know it.'

Of former Conservative MP Terence Clark, he said: 'He was the nearest thing to Neanderthal man on the Tory benches.'

In his later years, Healey has been rather more even-handed, being just as insulting to Labour politicians as he is to those in other parties. Of Labour heavyweight Dick Crossman, he said: 'A large man with spectacles, mousy hair falling lank on each side of his forehead, and a mouth which turned down at the corners with the expression of Burglar Bill in the dock. He had a heavyweight intellect with a lightweight judgement. As a politician and even more as a minister, he left much to be desired.'

Commenting on former Labour colleagues, Healey said of Chris Mayhew: 'He was something of a boy scout, seeing issues always in black and white.' And Philip Noel-Baker he dismissed, saying: 'I found him louche and slovenly.'

Some of Healey's most biting insults are directed at his former colleague and one-time party leader and Prime Minister, Harold Wilson. Among other things he has said of Wilson: 'He did not have political principle ... He had no sense of direction and rarely looked more than a few months ahead ... He had short-term opportunism allied with a capacity for self delusion, which made Walter Mitty appear unimaginative ... When things went wrong he imagined everyone was conspiring against him ... As his domestic worries increased, Wilson found that dabbling in foreign affairs was a distraction no less enjoyable for being futile.'

Healey on newspaper magnate Cecil King: 'He was an outsized man both in physique, ambition and in self esteem.'

On Tony Benn: 'His ministerial career has left only

Denis Healey

two monuments behind: the uranium mine in Namibia he authorized as Energy Secretary, which helps to support apartheid and is in territory illegally occupied by South Africa; and Concorde, an aircraft which is used by wealthy people on their expense accounts, whose fares are subsidized by much poorer taxpayers.

'Benn was a worthy successor to the Cripps of the 1930s. The phenomenon they represent has something in common with that feudal Socialism which Marx and Engels described in the Communist manifesto as far back as 1848 – half lamentation and half lampoon – half echo of the past, half menace of the future. It was Tony Benn's total incapacity to understand the march of modern history which ensured that when he came close to capturing the Party machine, he came close to destroying the Labour Party as a force in twentieth-century British politics.'

Healey on Tory Harold Macmillan: 'An unscrupulous opportunist and a brilliant actor. His air of Edwardian languor enabled him to get away with innumerable deceptions and political somersaults without ever being detected.' He went on to say that, later, the Labour Party produced a Macmillan of its own in Harold Wilson.

His view on former American President Lyndon Johnson: 'He exuded a brutal lust for power which I found most disagreeable. He boasted acting on the principle "Give me a man's balls and his heart and mind will follow." He was a monster.'

Commenting on President Nasser of Egypt: 'He suffered from *le démon du bien*; he simply could not resist a flattering temptation.'

On former American President, Jimmy Carter: 'He was a moral puritan and an economic profligate.'

On Michael Foot: 'He lacked both the personal authority and the political grip to impose his will as party leader. He was a natural rebel and found leadership uncongenial; moreover, though a brilliant orator, he had no administrative experience or executive ability.'

Commenting on Lord Joseph (the former Conservative Cabinet minister, Sir Keith Joseph), he said: 'He is a mixture of Hamlet, Rasputin and Tommy Cooper.'

Of the former deputy leader of the Labour Party, George Brown, he said: 'Like the immortal Jemima, when he was good, he was very very good, but when he was bad he was horrid . . . He carried an enormous chip on his shoulder which tended to make him jealous of anyone with a university education. An appalling bully.'

As I've mentioned earlier, Churchill once remarked that Clement Attlee was a modest man with a lot to be modest about. A Tory back-bencher, with a grudging respect for Healey's ability, was heard recently saying of him: 'He is a vain man – with a lot to be vain about.'

GEORGE THOMAS, former Speaker of the House of Commons and now Lord Tonypandy, said of Healey: 'He has the most wonderful gift of vituperation.'

ALTHOUGH SHE was no doubt trying to be helpful, a BBC make-up girl, in 1963, delivered a telling insult to Sir Alec Douglas-Home, then Prime Minister.

Sir Alec had asked her if she could make him look any better on television. She said no, and Sir Alec asked why not. The girl told him it was because he had a head like a skull. Sir Alec asked, 'Hasn't everybody?' She said, 'No,' and that, according to Sir Alec, was the end of the conversation.

Sir Alec's views on President Gorbachev of Russia: 'He is a Lenin fundamentalist. He is enigmatic. He has gathered a reputation for liberalism, but at the same time has arrogated to himself, in the office of President, powers which a Stalin would envy.'

THROUGHOUT HIS political career, James Callaghan has projected a friendly, avuncular image – he's not so much a father figure as a 'friendly uncle'. His style in the Commons was rarely insulting – soothing and soporific would be a more accurate way to describe how he handled his critics. However, even Jim was ruffled by the Turkish Foreign Minister, Turan Gunes, whom he regarded as an expert at obstruction – Gunes once held up a meeting for several hours as he elaborated his objections to the name plates around the conference table.

When, years later, Callaghan was asked his view on the Turkish minister Gunes, he said: 'He was a dark loquacious character who looked somewhat like Groucho Marx but without the humour.'

On Enoch Powell: 'He fanned prejudice to fever heat.'

WILLIAM WHITELAW, now Lord Whitelaw, was Deputy Prime Minister and Leader of the House of Lords until ill health forced him to retire a few years ago. He remains a popular figure in the Conservative Party. In the last parliament he taunted the leaders of the Labour Party: 'The loony left are always hovering in the wing. They have a loony defence policy and a loony economic policy and, in the main, when they appear on television, they look pretty loony themselves.'

Recalling a disaster early in his political career, when he was fighting a rough seat during the 1950 election, Lord Whitelaw tells of a government minister speaking for him when a man in the audience shouted, 'Liar.' 'Who said that?' demanded the pompous politician. 'I did, and I'll say it again,' said the heckler. 'Liar!' To

Whitelaw's horror, the main speaker replied, 'If you say that again, I will speak no more.' Timing his intervention brilliantly, the heckler waited for about five minutes and then shouted again, 'Liar!' The minister turned to Lord Whitelaw and said 'I shall go and leave this rabble to you. Goodbye.' Lord Whitelaw recalls that he never again saw the minister, whose career did not prosper either. At that stage, neither did William Whitelaw's; he lost the seat.

BEFORE TERRY DICKS became Member of Parliament for Hayes and Harlington, he stood, unsuccessfully, as the Tory candidate in Bristol East where the sitting Labour MP was Michael Cocks.

Michael, on being asked the difference between the candidates, replied: 'Some of the electorate might think they've got no choice – it's either Cocks or Dicks.'

Shortly after the 1983 election, when Cocks was Labour Chief Whip in the Commons, he went into the government Whip's office, to clarify some item of business. Waiting for the arrival of the Tory Chief Whip, he sat in a government Whip's chair, when a young Tory MP, just elected to the House, timidly peeped around the door. Cocks was sitting in the office alone and the new boy began, hesitantly, to address him. 'I wondered if I could be excused from voting tomorrow so I can attend my son's christening?' the new MP asked. 'You bloody shit!' Michael Cocks bellowed, 'You've only been here five minutes and already you're asking for time off. Piss off and don't let me see you again!' 'Sorry sir,' the new MP meekly piped as he quickly disappeared. A few minutes later, roars of laughter were heard from Michael Cocks.

LORD JOSEPH, formerly a Cabinet minister, is a Tory

right-winger. He views the policies of consensus that were pursued by former Conservative Prime Ministers Macmillan and Heath as a disaster which failed to stem the tide of Socialism. As the Labour Party moved further to the left, Sir Keith pointed out that, in their pursuit of the middle ground, the Tories had been virtually helping them. Taking a swipe at the party 'wets' he said: 'On the road to Socialism, the Conservative Party has, in the past, been an accessory after-the-fact.'

LABOUR POLITICIAN Richard Crossman, who died in 1974, held a number of his colleagues in contempt, regarding himself as one of the few original thinkers: 'One of the difficulties of politics is that politicians are shocked by those who are really prepared to let their thinking reach any conclusion. "Political thinking" consists in deciding on the conclusions first and then finding good arguments for them. An open mind is considered irresponsible.'

And, commenting on his own party: 'Whenever I am lectured on the virtues of moderation in Labour politics, I feel as Hermann Goering did about culture and reach for my revolver.'

MARGARET THATCHER, Britain's first woman Prime Minister, has become one of the longest serving Prime Ministers of all time. Elected Conservative leader in 1975, she has led the Conservatives to victory at three consecutive General Elections – 1979, 1983 and 1987. This, by any reckoning, is a remarkable record which is unlikely to be matched by any other politician in her lifetime. She was regarded by many political observers as something of an unknown quantity when she challenged Edward Heath for the Tory leadership after his general election defeat of 1974, having held only the relatively junior Cabinet position of Secretary of State for Education. It was not long after she entered Downing Street, however, that it became clear she was not going to be a 'soft touch' for anyone. One of the first pieces of invective aimed at her from overseas was turned by the Prime Minister from being an insulting gibe to being a comment on her steadfastness. The 'Iron Lady' crack from the Russians has stuck, but not in the way the Soviets had intended.

However, she has not always had things all her own way. A decade earlier, when she was Education Minister, she withdrew free school milk causing the Parliamentary Labour Party to coin what was actually the first insulting nickname of her career: 'Milk-snatcher.'

In the Commons, and on public platforms, she has not been afraid to express herself in the strongest possible terms.

In opposition, she silenced a Labour government minister with: 'The honourable gentleman suffers from the fact that I understand him perfectly.'

She has summed up the majority of her colleagues with: 'One of the things being in politics has taught me is that men are not a reasoned or reasonable sex.'

In 1974, she scored a notable hit in the Commons with her attack on Labour's finance spokesman, Harold Lever, about whom she said: 'There are four ways of acquiring money – make it, earn it, marry it and borrow it. Mr. Lever seems to know about all four.'

In October 1980, a number of journalists sneeringly pointed out that she would have to change the economic course of her government as things were looking rather bleak. Her reply was characteristically blunt and contained a hint of a side-swipe at former Prime Minister Edward Heath, who himself had made a number of changes in policy when the going got tough: 'To those waiting with bated breath for that favourite media

catchphrase, the U-turn, I have only one thing to say –
U turn if you want to, the lady's not for turning.'

In 1984, Mrs Thatcher did not shrink from describing
some European leaders as 'ostriches', for not realizing
the need for changes in the agricultural structure of the
EEC.

When the announcement was made in 1988 of an
alliance between the Liberal and SDP Parties, her
response was characteristic: 'They have a new colour –
they call it gold. It looks like yellow to me.'

And commenting on Neil Kinnock: 'He is a crypto-
communist'.

Apparently, the French President Giscard d'Estaing,
when in office, used to describe Margaret Thatcher as
'La fille de l'épicier' (the grocer's daughter). Although
this was clearly intended to be insulting, and was only
spoken behind her back, it is doubtful if the Prime
Minister would have felt affronted. Even today, she
takes pride in the lessons of thrift and hard work that
she learnt from her father. In any event, according to
one journalist, Mrs Thatcher was inclined to describe
Giscard himself as 'a bogus Count'.

President Mitterand of France may not quite have
Giscard's grand manner but some would say he has a
better turn of phrase. His view of our first woman Prime
Minister is that: 'She has the mouth of Marilyn Monroe,
and the eyes of Caligula.'

Her career as Britain's Prime Minister came spectacu-
larly to an end when she failed to win outright in the
first ballot for the Conservative Party leadership in November 1990. A Prime Minister who had never been
defeated at the ballot box by the public was ousted by
her own parliamentary colleagues. During the leadership election, she said of her challenger, Michael Heseltine: 'He is all glamour and no substance.'

Perhaps the best *bon mot* was coined by Labour left-
winger, Dennis Skinner, who was asked by a tabloid

journalist if he would comment on the first ballot of the Tory leadership election race when the only candidates were Thatcher and Heseltine. Skinner said there was not much point, as both of the candidates were identical. When asked what he meant by this remark, Skinner reposted: 'They are both millionaires – and they are both peroxide blondes.'

JOHN MAJOR'S political rise has been nothing short of meteoric. He only entered Parliament in 1979 and yet by 1990, he was in 10 Downing Street. He won the ballot for the Conservative leadership election following the withdrawal of Margaret Thatcher from the race.

His quiet and pleasant manner belies a shrewd and clever politician. However, the difference in style between him and his predecessor could not be more marked.

For a number of years, tabloid journalists were telling the British public that Margaret Thatcher was too bossy and that she failed to consult with her Cabinet and with other colleagues. Rather oddly, the same journalists, only a few months later, began criticising John Major for taking time to consult, saying this was 'indecision and dither'.

Those who know John Major well know he is not a ditherer, but sees the advantages in assessing the weight of argument on an issue.

Just after he entered Downing Street, the press featured many articles highlighting John Major's humble background. After a few weeks of press coverage on this subject, a Tory backbencher was overheard to remark: 'I cannot stand his lowlier-than-thou attitude.'

John Major has said, of Labour's John Smith: 'He has as much likelihood of understanding how the economy works as Donald Duck has of winning Mastermind.'

On making a maiden speech: 'Making a maiden

speech is rather like having a baby – it is terrible beforehand, it is an awful effort during delivery, but one gets a marvellous night's sleep afterwards.'

Commenting on Michael Foot he said: 'His idea of a policy is to spend, spend, spend. He is the Viv Nicholson of politics.'

And again on Michael Foot: 'Whatever has gone wrong with the country in the past, he blames on the government. I suspect if he caught measles, he would claim that he caught it from the Treasury Bench.'

Brushing aside a Labour call for lower interest rates, John Major silenced Labour criticism with the jibe: 'Soft options usually lead to hard times.'

And taking a swipe at the former actor, Labour MP Andrew Faulds, he said: 'Fresh from his triumph as Carver Doone, he interrupts us again having woken from his slumbers. It was one of the worst auditions that I have ever heard.'

And referring to Labour's industrial strategy under Neil Kinnock: 'Instead of a national plan, Labour will now have a medium term industrial strategy. . . . instead of George Brown, we shall have Gordon Brown – otherwise it is all the same.'

Of a Labour backbencher, who was frequently out of his depth: 'The Honourable gentleman had an expensive education. I am not sure it was money well spent. I had the doubtful privilege of paying taxes in order to keep him at university. Frankly, I would like my money back.'

On Labour's Dennis Skinner: 'He frequently sees things that others cannot. If he had been at the Walls of Jericho when they fell, he would have blamed the government for poor maintenance. He needs a verbal straitjacket.'

On Labour's David Winnick: 'He greets every problem with an open mouth and a closed mind. He gave us an impersonation of a mixture of Uriah Heep and Jaws. He has about as much charm as a puff adder.'

On Labour's Energy Spokesman Frank Dobson: 'He behaves like an agitated parrot with constipation. He is the best advertisement I have yet seen for televising the House. Then people might see how he behaves. He is more funny than he is wise.'

On media presenter Robert Kilroy-Silk: 'He looks like a refugee from his sunlamp.'

LABOUR PARTY LEADER Neil Kinnock is no slouch when it comes to the delivery of an insult. He can be hard-hitting in debate, but does have a tendency to spoil the effect by his loquacity.

Of the now-defunct SDP, he said: 'They have policies like liquid grease.'

And commenting on Norman Fowler and Nigel Lawson, when they were both Cabinet ministers: 'Norman Fowler looks as if he is suffering from a famine and Lawson looks as though he caused it.'

His view of David Owen: 'He possesses an ego fat on arrogance and drunk on ambition.'

He once said of a performance by Mrs Thatcher that it resembled 'crocodile tears with crocodile teeth'.

Attacking Mrs Thatcher in the House, for her habit of using the royal 'we', he said, 'The Prime Minister says to the Commonwealth Conference that if it is forty-eight against one, "I feel sorry for the forty-eight", and she says to the European Summit when it is eleven to one, "I feel sorry for the eleven". From what we hear from the United States Secretary of State for Defense over the weekend, the Prime Minister may soon be saying to our NATO allies that she feels sorry for the other fifteen. When I hear the Prime Minister feeling sorry for the rest of the world, I understand why she has taken to calling herself "We" – it is less lonely that way.'

During the 1983 general election campaign, shortly after the Falklands conflict, when a reporter asked Mr Kinnock at least to admit that Mrs Thatcher has guts, he responded, 'It's a pity that people have to leave theirs on Goose Green in order to prove it.' This remark backfired badly and caused a major outcry at the time, particularly from families of servicemen who had been casualties of the Falklands War. The incident prompted Michael Heseltine to remark that Kinnock was 'the self-appointed King of the Gutter'. The use of insults while electioneering always requires a degree of restraint. Mr Kinnock should have remembered the outcry against fellow Welshman Nye Bevan when he made his 'vermin' gibe, and known better.

LIBERAL-DEMOCRAT heavyweight Sir Cyril Smith can be quite effective, both in debate and in the media. He definitely has the common touch and his remarks are usually 'punchy' and frequently carry more bite than those of his party's spokesmen, one of whom is so long-winded that he frequently empties the Commons chamber when he rises to speak.

Smith's view of Tony Benn: 'He did more harm to British industry in one speech than the combined efforts of the Luftwaffe and the U-boats did in the whole of the last War.'

On Nigel Lawson, when he was Chancellor of the Exchequer: 'He reminds me of King Canute.'

By all accounts, he is very popular in his constituency, except perhaps with pop star Lisa Stansfield. She also hails from Rochdale and, when asked what her town had got, replied: 'We've got Cyril Smith who's so fat he takes up most of the f**king town.'

NIGEL LAWSON may not be widely regarded as a charismatic politician, or as someone who excites with his oratory, but he has one of the best brains in politics and is a very shrewd operator. His decision to retire from politics at the next election will be a big loss to the Conservatives. In debate, when he is on form, he can be devastating. His style is very much in the manner of 'why use a mallet when a sledgehammer will do'. In this vein is his comment on the Liberals' decision in the 1970s to form the Lib-Lab pact to maintain the Labour government in office: 'It is the only time in history that rats have been known to join a sinking ship.'

On Neil Kinnock he has said, 'He has an infallible knack for getting the wrong end of every stick.'

When, during a speech in the Commons, he was interrupted by Labour MP David Winnick, he brushed him aside with a wave of his hand and the crack: 'He is a conspicuous example of one of the less salubrious Members of Parliament.' I do not know who it was who said, 'When in a hole, stop digging,' but Mr Winnick should have heeded this advice. He made matters far worse by raising a point of order with the Speaker, complaining about Nigel Lawson's insult: 'I am sometimes criticized by my colleagues for the fact that I rarely drink. Should not the Chancellor apologize for his slur?' The Speaker appeared as surprised as the rest of the House, responding with, 'Order. I do not think that the word "salubrious" has anything to do with drink.' Winnick subsided to howls of derisive laughter from the government benches.

Lawson also remarked bitingly of Labour's education proposals: 'The difference between their extremists and their moderates is that the extremists want to abolish private education now, the moderates want to wait until their own children have finished school.'

He has, of course, been a fair target for insults himself and not only from members of the opposition. During his period as a Government minister, he was rather insultingly nicknamed 'Niglet' by the then Tory MP Norman St John-Stevas. On one occasion seeing Lawson enter the chamber in a cream suit, one Tory back-bencher (who prefers to be nameless) described him as 'looking like an Armenian might whilst on holiday in Florida'.

A story is told of an occasion some months ago when Nigel went to have his hair cut and generously handed the barber a 50p tip.

Far from being grateful, the barber remonstrated with Mr Lawson, pointing out that he had been given an Irish coin. Lawson is alleged to have retorted: 'Oh well, put it in a parking meter then,' before disappearing out of the shop.

UNLIKE NIGEL LAWSON, the Labour MP Bill Stones was not known for his intellect. Indeed, he was so thick that he probably thought that a piano-forte was a motorway café. He did, however, seem to be conscious of his own limitations as well as those of his electors when he endearingly said, 'There's a lot of bleeding idiots in the country, and they deserve some representation.'

ON THE other hand, no one can deny the intellect of Enoch Powell, once a Tory and then an Ulster Unionist MP, who said, after leaving his former party, 'There is one thing you can be sure of with the Conservative Party, before anything else – they have a grand sense for where the votes are.'

Some would say that he later spoke his own epitaph when he remarked 'all political careers end in failure'.

On one occasion, the former Labour MP Leo Abse was having a flaming row with Enoch on the subject of

Nigel Lawson.

Ulster, and whether British troops should stay there. Overhearing this, an MP commented that the two men held each other in mutual contempt. 'Yes,' another MP agreed, 'and they're both right.'

CABINET MINISTER Kenneth Clarke, never at a loss for a punchy answer, surprised some of his colleagues with his frankness when he said, 'If I had to say which was telling the truth about society, a speech by a Minister of Housing, or the actual buildings put up in his time, I should believe the buildings.'

After a debate on health, he observed: 'In politics, the more caring the subject, the rougher the debate.'

TONY BENN has been a leading figure in the Labour Party for nearly thirty years. The left-winger has always been a controversial figure, even in his own party. To the amusement of some Tories, as his career has progressed, his name, rather oddly, has shortened. Lord Stansgate renounced his hereditary peerage to become Anthony Wedgwood-Benn. Mr Wedgwood-Benn then dropped one half of his Christian name, and the hyphen, to become the plainer-sounding 'Tony Benn'.

'The former peer is trying to pretend that he is a common working man,' some Tories have ribbed. Whatever one calls him, he is an excellent orator, frequently speaking at length in the Commons without the aid of notes. When he wants to be insulting, he can be remarkably effective.

Commenting on Neil Kinnock: 'He is not a substantial person. He is a media figure.'

On Harold Wilson: 'Most of his speeches are cheap, but he gets away with it. He is the old entertainer – the Archie Rice of the Labour Party.'

On journalist Peter Jenkins: 'I thoroughly dislike him

– he is a real decayed gossip columnist of the Gaitskell variety.'

On former Labour MP Bill Rodgers (who went on to form the now defunct SDP): 'He is an intolerable man – but is also a great fighter.'

His view on the state of Britain today: 'The country is suffering from galloping obsolescence.'

CECIL PARKINSON, former Conservative Party Chairman, is an urbane and polished debater, who can make even the most hard-hitting gibe sound civilized, if not complimentary. His manner is extremely effective on television as well as in the Commons chamber.

A good example of his style are his comments on Labour's Shadow Transport Minister, John Prescott, of whom he said: 'His attempt to make political capital out of every dreadful tragedy is both offensive and malicious. To claim that the Lockerbie air crash was a symbol of government cost-cutting just shows how low the modern Labour Party will stoop in the search for votes. Well I can tell John Prescott, the only person who will fall for that electoral pitch will be the terrorist who planted the bomb.' He went on to add: 'John Prescott is a political vulture and his desire to be seen on television verges on the obscene.'

However, Mr Parkinson does not have it all his own way. John Prescott himself has said of Mr Parkinson (although hardly with the same élan): 'He is a nutter. His remarks are those of an exhausted minister.' Rather better was Prescott's junior spokesman, Peter Snape, who commented: 'Parkinson's red face looming over the dispatch-box is a pretty terrifying sight. I was not sure at one stage whether it was indignation, claret, or a faulty sun-lamp.'

DAVID OWEN, the former leader of the now defunct

SDP, does not now seem to have his heart in politics, particularly since he announced that he is to retire at the next election. However, he has recently said of his one-time Labour colleague Roy Hattersley: 'He is the acceptable face of opportunism.'

And David Owen's view of Margaret Thatcher: 'She is a heady mixture of whisky and perfume.'

TRADE SECRETARY Peter Lilley became quite irate during one debate when his comments were misrepresented by Labour back-bencher Tony Worthington who, before he entered politics, used to work at a Borstal institution. So rattled was the minister by the Labour MP's speech that he retorted: 'I know that he was for a period an inmate of Borstal. I am sorry that he learnt more from its inhabitants than he was able to teach them.'

LADY FALKENDER commenting on former Social Services Secretary John Moore, 'His delivery at the dispatch-box has all the bite of a rubber duck.'

DURING HIS period as Transport Minister, Paul Channon was asked about the difficulties of the job. He replied: 'The trouble with being Secretary of State for Transport is that it is the only job I know where you are expected to apologize to others when they are late for your meetings.'

A YEAR before the demise of the Social Democrats, Kenneth Baker, the Home Secretary, accurately predicted the way things were moving; he said of David Owen, then SDP Leader: 'I saw David Owen on television the other week. He was heckling a small number of bystanders in Torquay. And then I realized they weren't bystanders – they were his party.'

When James Callaghan resigned the leadership of the Labour Party and Michael Foot was elected, Kenneth Baker was heard to comment: 'The Labour Party was led by Dixon of Dock Green. Now it is being led by Worzel Gummidge.'

In the earlier Labour leadership election, when Harold Wilson had announced he was standing down, Roy Hattersley decided that he would give his support to Jim Callaghan, who was in fact the eventual winner. As two of his friends, Roy Jenkins and Tony Crosland, were also standing, he thought he would do the honourable thing and inform them.

He first of all went to see Roy Jenkins at the Home Office and explained his deep respect for him, but said that in the interests of the party unity, he would be voting for Callaghan. Apparently, Jenkins listened sympathetically, and the two men then enjoyed a drink before Hattersley left.

Pleased with this civilized meeting, Hattersley then went to the Department of the Environment where Tony Crosland was Secretary of State. He again explained his reasoning, spoke of the difficulty of his choice and said that he would have to vote for Callaghan. Crosland, at the end of this long explanation, drew on his cigar and said: 'Thank you, Roy, for your honesty and candour in coming to see me and telling me this. I appreciate it greatly. Now piss off.'

A Tory backbencher commenting on Labour's Roy Hattersley: 'He can only be described as an area of outstanding national humbug.'

MINISTER OF STATE at the Home Office, John

Patten, has a bouncy and good natured style in the Commons and is rarely insulting. However, during the Committee stage of the Criminal Justice Bill, in 1990, he did become rather irritated with two of the Labour Party's Home Affairs spokesmen, Messrs Barry Sheerman and Stuart Randall, causing him, in a rare display of bile to describe the Labour team as 'a couple of shellbacks – they are like two middle-aged mutant turtles.'

ONE OF the most acid-tongued politicians of the twentieth century is undoubtedly Norman Tebbit. Among his many barbs of invective, the following are the most memorable:

'I have never rated Neil Kinnock as anything but a windbag whose incoherent speeches spring from an incoherent mind.'

Again on Kinnock: 'He has a proven inability to conceal his immaturity when under pressure.'

On the SLD: 'Liberals are Enid Blyton Socialists – a dustbin for undecided votes.'

'Lord Soper has always appeared to me to be the epitome of sanctimonious ill-judgement.'

On Ted Heath's premiership: 'Events have shown that the Heath government rarely persisted with any of its announced policies once the going got rough – except on Europe.'

When someone said that Socialism was dead, Tebbit disagreed. 'It's not dead, just brain-dead,' he replied.

On Labour MP David Winnick: 'I can never quite understand why he walks that way. He either has a bad tailor or he has filled his pants.'

And Tebbit on Labour spokesman Frank Dobson: 'He's gutless and does not know what he is talking about.'

To a journalist: 'Those who scream and throw eggs

are not the real unemployed. If they were really hard up, they would be eating them.'

Commenting on the change in image of the Labour Party: 'The voters are not daft. They can smell a rat whether it is wrapped in a red flag or covered in roses.'

While campaigning in support of Jeremy Hanley, Norman Tebbit was addressing a public meeting when a youth at the back started heckling him. Norman Tebbit tried to soothe matters by saying 'Calm down, my lad,' to which the youth shouted, 'You're not my dad.' Mr Tebbit silenced his barracking completely with his response. 'I would quit while you're ahead, son. It's obvious I'm the only father you'll ever know.'

'What is the difference between a scud missile and British Rail?' Norman recently asked a Conservative Backbencher. The MP looked nonplussed. 'I don't know,' he replied. He was rather shocked by the Tebbit retort: 'More people have been killed by British Rail.'

Former Labour Cabinet minister and MP, Eric Varley, said of him, 'Putting Norman Tebbit in charge of industrial relations is like appointing Dracula to take charge of the blood transfusion service.'

The *Observer* perhaps most accurately described Norman Tebbit: 'The American adage "don't get mad, get even" doesn't apply to Norman. He gets mad *and* even.'

And a fairly typical comment about Norman Tebbit (from a Conservative back-bencher): 'If a wasp flew into Norman's mouth – he would sting it.'

TOM SWAIN, the former Labour MP, rarely spoke in the House. However, he was once moved to fits of rage by comments from Norman Tebbit. Swain shouted, 'If you say that outside, I'll punch your bloody head in!' A Conservative MP was heard to mutter that this was the most articulate speech Mr Swain had made in his seventeen years in the House!

ANDREW FAULDS has the best voice in Parliament. At least, that is his view. Actually, the former Thespian is probably right. Certainly, he never has difficulty in being heard.

His style in the House is unique. Rather than expound an argument in detail, via the vehicle of a lengthy speech, he assumes that the Tories *know* what he stands for. Of course, he *knows* what they stand for, and therefore time is saved for the real purpose of the sitting of Parliament: the bellowing of insults at each other.

It is, no doubt, Mr Faulds' previous experience on the stage that has provided him with both the knowledge and the inner resources for his distinctive approach. His method is rather akin to the manner of a Shakespearian actor auditioning for a crowd scene at a football match. He gets full marks for style but the content is usually less than salubrious (if Mr Winnick will forgive me).

However, his Westminster appearances are invariably amusing and someone always gets insulted. Once, when he was being barracked by Conservative back-benchers, he responded, 'This is a serious matter, even for the Girl Guides opposite.' The gibe led to an unidentified female shouting, 'There's nothing wrong with Girl Guides.' Irritated with all this levity, Mr Faulds responded with the rather equivocal line: 'Perhaps I have known more Girl Guides than the honourable lady.' He did not help to prevent the rising level of amusement by then going on to say that he wished to talk about some of his 'recent experiences', causing loud laughter from the Conservative benches. Exasperated, Mr Faulds turned his tongue upon members of the Press Gallery whom he referred to as 'termites'. This tactic worked at once and the frivolity ceased. After all, MPs are well aware that a joke is a joke . . . but the Press is no laughing matter.

On another occasion, it was the former Chancellor of the Exchequer, Nigel Lawson, who caused Faulds to explode and refer to Lawson as a 'fat slug'.

Mr Faulds' displays of artistic temperament are not always directed at the Tories. In November 1988 he was so outraged at not being called by the Speaker during Foreign Office questions, that he slammed his papers on the bench, startling his colleagues, and then stormed out of the chamber shouting 'disgraceful' at the Speaker, and muttering something about the fact that he was trying to ask two questions and had twice not been called. He also gesticulated with two fingers at the Speaker. The most charitable interpretation of this was that he was reinforcing the point that he had twice tried to be called to ask a question.

THE DEFENCE MINISTER, Alan Clark, is known in the House for his rather languid and laid-back style.

During a debate on the Royal Air Force he was questioned as to whether he intended that women pilots should fly combat aircraft, or would they be kept strictly flying transport aircraft, or aircraft other than those in wartime use.

He put down his questioner with: 'Perhaps I am over-fastidious, perhaps I am old-fashioned, but I associate women's special gifts with activities other than the taking of life.'

And taking a swipe at the opposition defence spokesman, Allan Rogers, he said, 'When he is speaking spontaneously and with sincerity, then he is at his most effective and convincing. When he is reciting various items fed to him by a graduate of the Bradford Peace

Studies School, or whoever writes his research, he is rather less persuasive.'

His tongue frequently turns on the gentlemen of the Press: 'Journalists are extremely sensitive to any sort of attack, in contrast with the way in which they themselves behave – a characteristic of public life with which we are all familiar.'

And silencing Labour back-bencher Tam Dalyell he said, 'He asked a number of pertinent questions, and ended – characteristically and reassuringly, because we all like people to behave in character – with a highly idiosyncratic, if not batty, suggestion.'

EDWINA CURRIE is probably one of the most insulted politicians of modern times. Some would say she deserves all she gets in this respect because of what they regard as her pushy and attention-seeking manner.

Before she was appointed a minister, I shared a tiny office with Edwina and found her at all times to be courteous, helpful and friendly. She is an intelligent lady who has been on the receiving end of some downright unjustified insults. During the 1983 Parliament, gibes at Edwina's expense were at their height and the Press, never slow to follow a trend, happily joined in.

On one occasion in 1984 I returned to our office to find a lone uninvited journalist looking through the papers on Edwina's desk. He made some unconvincing excuse as to what he was doing and then hurriedly left. I later reported the incident to Edwina, who could have had the journalist thrown out of Westminster for such outrageous behaviour. Instead, she just shrugged her shoulders and muttered something about being 'fair game for the diary columnists'. She went on to add that there was nothing worth revealing on her desk in any event.

I must say that – apart from a collection of photographs on her notice board, showing Edwina attending various functions – I could not see anything that could be of interest to the Press. Her desk, like mine, contained just a bundle of parliamentary papers.

A few days later, a diary piece appeared to the effect that Edwina was so impressed with her own abilities that she had no fewer than five photographs of herself pinned up in her room. To my surprise, the report went on to say: 'Her room-mate Greg Knight meanwhile has only one photograph on his notice board – and this is of a monkey. Is he trying to tell her something?'*

The same newspaper, a few months later, ran a further diary piece nominating me for 'the Patience of the Saint of the Year Award' for 'going beyond the call of duty and sharing an office with Edwina Currie'.

I mention these incidents (there are more) to show that many of the stories that have been circulated about Edwina did not arise, as some believe, at her own instigation. In any event, Edwina has also shown that, when it comes to insults, she is certainly able to dish it out.

A couple of years ago, she infuriated many Labour MPs with a swipe not only at Neil Kinnock, but also at his wife when she said: 'Neil is ruled by the person who makes him breakfast.'

And on the Liberal candidate during a by-election in West Derbyshire: 'He is a pompous prat.'

Continuing to display what some would call her typical Northern bluntness, she once suggested that the Poet Laureate, Ted Hughes, should 'sod off'.

On fellow Conservative MP, Teresa Gorman: 'Small, short-sighted, blond, barbed – she reminds me of a bright little hedgehog.'

---

* The facts were true. At the time I was the owner of a squirrel monkey called Ben and his photograph was pinned on my notice-board.

On Harriet Harman, Labour health spokesman: 'Pedestrian and predictable.'

On Labour MP David Hinchliffe: 'His manner is cheerful, but his appearance is close to that of a garden gnome without the woolly hat. His politics are somewhat to the left of Fidel Castro.'

Her view on Labour MP Robin Cook: 'He is leprechaun-like.'

However, the delivery of an insult can need forethought. Though she effectively insulted Derbyshire MP Dennis Skinner by her comment on him 'Derbyshire born, Derbyshire bred, strong of arm and thick in the head', the barb went wide. Although Mr Skinner was insulted, so too were many of Edwina's voters – she too represents a Derbyshire seat! This is one insult which, come the next election, she may regret.

Being a controversial figure has meant that most of the insults directed at Edwina have been deliberate, but on one occasion she was insulted unintentionally by a well-meaning member of the public. During the summer of 1989, Edwina attended the Chelsea Flower Show and, as she expected, it was not long before she was recognized. A rather elderly lady came over to her, caught her arm and started chatting away, saying how pleased she was that they had bumped into each other and generally making polite and complimentary conversation. This, of course, was no more than Edwina had expected. Then, suddenly, the old lady started talking about British Telecom and added, 'I must tell you how much I enjoy those ads.' At this point, Edwina became rather suspicious. 'Ads?' she inquired. 'Excuse me, but who do you think I am?' To which the old dear replied, 'I know who you are – you're Maureen Lipman!' Although no insult was intended, Edwina was certainly stung.

And her view of her compatriots: 'The main effect of alcohol is to release inhibitions. As we have drinking and driving, football hooliganism, battered wives and children, and carousing and violence in the streets, we British must at heart be a collection of noisy and aggressive slobs.'

In the light of her experience since entering public life, Edwina would probably agree with Charlotte Whitton, a former mayor of Ottawa, who said, 'Whatever women do they must do twice as well as men to be thought half as good. Luckily this is not difficult.'

Just before her resignation, fellow Conservative MP, Robin Maxwell-Hyslop called Edwina 'a junior minister with an uncontrollable tongue and an insatiable desire to self advertisement'.

Bearded Labour MP Frank Dobson caused much amusement when reference was made in a debate to Edwina Currie going to have her teeth examined. He suggested: 'When she goes to the dentist, he's the one who needs the anaesthetic.'

A politician should never assume that his remarks will go unreported. When Conservative MP Andrew MacKay attended a private function, he made a crack about Edwina: 'She has done for our party what King Herod did for babysitting.' He merely expected the quip to enliven his speech. However, a journalist was in the audience and the joke appeared in the William Hickey column. In cold print it read like a vicious insult.

Richard Holt is a hard-working Tory MP who has, in the past, had disagreements with Edwina, about whom he once said 'her only interest is publicity', adding: 'Edwina Currie is to the Conservative Party what the Bishop of Durham is to the Church of England.'

Holt's no-nonsense style frequently upsets the opposition. He gives as good as he gets in debate, frequently barracking Labour left-winger Dennis Skinner. When Militant-backed MP Dave Nellist left some guests on the Terrace of the House of Commons (against the rules) Holt demanded that they be removed, adding for good measure, that they were 'a load of scum'.

Tony Beaumont-Dark, the Member of Parliament for Birmingham Selly Oak, has also taken a swipe at Mrs C. He said, 'I don't think anyone is afraid of Edwina Currie – except perhaps Mr Currie.' And, asked if Mrs Currie should rejoin the government, 'I don't think so. Junior ministers are there to do the bidding. They are not very successful if they explode like Chinese crackers all over the place. In Edwina's case, it is the Chinese cracker syndrome – and there are enough ministers in government already who are crackers.'

DURING HIS long ministerial career, Nicholas Ridley has made many friends at Westminster, but even those opposed to him could not deny his individual and somewhat languid but effective style.

During one particular debate in the Commons, the Labour MP Tony Banks was becoming rather excitable: 'When can we expect an announcement?' he demanded. Then, for effect, Mr Banks waxed colourful: 'I have twice brought my sponge-bag and twice I have returned home early. My wife clearly thinks that I am having an unsuccessful affair.'

Mr Ridley was unimpressed and stone-faced. 'I really do not think that I can be held responsible for the disappointment to Mrs Banks.'

When Norman Fowler, one of his Cabinet colleagues, resigned from the government to spend more time with his family, someone asked Mr Ridley whether he was likely to pursue a similar course. 'Certainly not,' he responded, adding that he enjoyed being in government because he wished to spend 'less time' with *his* family.

Labour spokesman Gordon Brown made a reference to the Ridley style when he accused him of seeking to dismantle the Department of Trade and Industry. He quipped: 'Eventually, he will be seated alone at his desk; no in-tray, no out-tray . . . just an ashtray.'

But Mr Ridley's style is not everyone's cup of tea. Labour MP Martin Flannery has called Ridley's manner 'arrogant' adding, 'He is the only man in the world who can strut sitting down.'

ONE OF the main parliamentary interests of London Labour MP Tony Banks is the subject of the arts. This frequently puts him on a collision course with Conservative MP Terry Dicks, who is against using taxpayers' money for such a purpose. This has led to a good deal of Banks's invective being aimed at the Tory, the most memorable of which is: 'He is to the arts what James "Bonecrusher" Smith is to lepidoptery. His views are philistine in the extreme, anachronistic and wholly unacceptable to any civilized body of thought.'

In a later arts debate, in February 1990, Banks said: 'Listening to him opining on the arts is rather like listening to Vlad the Impaler presenting "Blue Peter". He is undoubtedly living proof that a pig's bladder on a stick can be elected as a Member of Parliament.' And Banks on Tory back-bencher Hugo Summerson: 'He looks like Neville Chamberlain's PPS.'

And his views of the Liberal Democrats: 'Woollyhatted, muesli-eating, Tory lick-spittles.'

In similar style, he expressed his view of Margaret Thatcher: 'She is happier getting in and out of tanks than in and out of museums or theatre seats. She seems to derive more pleasure from admiring new missiles than great works of art. What else can we expect from an ex-Spam hoarder from Grantham presiding over the social and economic decline of our country?'

TERRY DICKS has carved quite a niche for himself on

the subject of the arts. Indeed, he has described himself as the *only* opposition spokesman on the subject. His tirades against public subsidy have led to his being severely criticized, not just by Labour's Tony Banks, but by MPs from all parties. Nevertheless, in his assaults on what he calls the 'arty-farty' world, he has achieved the rare distinction of being one of the few MPs who causes the Chamber to fill when his name appears on the monitor screens. Among his broadsides are the following:

On opera: 'What is or is not art is a matter for personal choice. If some people want to listen to an overweight Italian singing in his own language, so be it. Am I supposed to believe that a man prancing about at the Royal Ballet in a pair of tights is part of my heritage? We have an Arts Minister. Why, I do not know. It is a matter of supply and demand. It is almost as bad as having a Minister for Sport.'

And on a similar theme: 'Subsidy for the arts is upper-crust nonsense.'

And again, on the arts: 'Avant garde usually means "'aven't a bean"'.

On his *bête noire*, Labour's Tony Banks: 'He is a man whose contribution to the arts is about the same as Bluebeard's contribution to the institution of marriage.'

Art-lover and fellow Conservative MP Patrick Cormack frequently feels the lash of Terry Dicks's tongue. Among other things, he has been called 'a pompous twit', and blasted with: 'He reminds me of Henry VIII – not with all the doublet and hose, but at least well-fed.'

Mr Dicks has also expressed his view on Dr Runcie, the former Archbishop of Canterbury: 'His contribution to Christianity could be written in longhand on a pinhead and still leave room for the Lord's Prayer.'

Dicks on former Indian leader Rajiv Gandhi: 'The

so-called leader of the world's largest democracy struts like a bloated peacock on the international stage.'

During a visit of Queen Noor of Jordan to Britain, following that country's ambivalent stand during the Gulf crisis, Conservative Terry Dicks commented: 'I think she's come to London to get a pair of pliers to get the splinters out of her husband's backside, he's sat on the fence for so long. I think the little wretch should stay out of this country and keep his family with him.'

However, Mr Dicks himself has been described by one political journalist as being 'like Arthur Mullard without the charm'.

RETURNING THE insult from Terry Dicks, Patrick Cormack has called him: 'Alf Garnett's vicar on earth – if ignorance is bliss, he must be an extremely happy man. What his constituents need most of all is a civilized Member of Parliament, and perhaps one day they will get one.'

IN 1987 the members of an overseas British parliamentary delegation were being bored by a particularly long-winded host who insisted on relating details of a serious accident he had suffered many years earlier and of how he was subsequently ill for ages. After he had been going on for over ten minutes about the one-time severity of his condition, the MP Dr John Blackburn silenced him with the query, 'And tell me, did you live?'

FORMER ARTS MINISTER and now Treasury Minister, David Mellor, well known for his hard-hitting style in the Commons, hit the mark when he insulted members of the Liberal-Democratic Alliance. 'None of the

Alliance's leaders are household names,' he commented, 'not even in their own home.'

On the abilities of another politician: 'She has a long reach but a short grasp.'

However, although Mr Mellor usually gets the best of a slanging match, he does not score on every occasion. Once during the passage of the Sexual Offences Bill, Mellor accused a back-bench MP Matthew Parris (who is now *The Times*'s sketch-writer) of 'conducting a debate with himself'. Parris replied, 'Maybe I am. But one has to have some kind of an intellectual challenge in this place.' Mr Parris did not stop at insulting Ministers of the Crown – he also insulted his own party workers. Once when taking part in a debate on the subject of prostitutes, Parris surprised the House by saying that he should have been attending a meeting of the West Derbyshire Conservative Ladies, but he made his apologies with the excuse that he was looking after their interests in the House.

IN 1989, whilst debating the future of Socialism, Tory MP Neil Hamilton sarcastically asked which minister would be answering the Debate, 'If not the Minister for Endangered Species, will it be the Trade Minister responsible for intellectual property, or the Minister responsible for bankruptcy? Perhaps they should both attend, as we are dealing with intellectual bankruptcy.'

On the Labour Party's policy review: 'We have been seeing a sort of Boston tea party with the Labour Party jettisoning electoral liabilities wherever they are discovered. Nowhere do we see this trickery more blatantly than with the Labour Party's defence policy. It has decided, supposedly, to drop its unilateral nuclear disarmament policy but the Leader of the Opposition remains a member of CND.'

And, developing his theme, Mr Hamilton suggested

that as they were updating their policies, the Labour Party should also update their anthem 'The Red Flag', suggesting the following:

> The people's flag is palest pink,
> We're not as red as you might think.
> So we can try and fight the polls,
> We've dumped our former left-wing goals.
>
> Ban the bomb? Not on your life!
> We'll outlaw strikes in place of strife.
> We'll keep your taxes well controlled,
> Free enterprise will be extolled.
>
> In office we'll reveal the trick,
> We'll tax and spend and live on tick.
> We'll nationalise smash and grab
> And City slickers we'll kebab.
>
> Though Labour's platform's total fudge,
> We are lefties still and will not budge.
> We're hoping you'll be taken in
> By Mandelson's PR machine.

And, his comment on seeing a bench full of Scottish Labour MPs: 'They are just like a group of grotesque gargoyles with balloon-like bodies.'

LABOUR STALWART and former minister, the late Eric Heffer, created quite a scene in the mid–80s when, due to his disagreement with his party leader, he stormed off the stage at his party conference as soon as Neil Kinnock rose to speak. He intended this to be insulting – as indeed it was. This led me to speculate during a speech, 'If Kinnock formed a government, what ministry would he offer Heffer? Perhaps he could be Minister for North Sea Oil Rigs,' I mused, on the basis that Kinnock might say, 'Let's see him try and walk off that platform!'

Heffer has in the past displayed a colourful turn of phrase. He described the Tory Party as 'Nothing else but a load of kippers – two-faced with no guts.'

His interventions are not always helpful to those he is trying to assist. When it was proposed that the Commons should suspend Labour MP Ron Brown, following his mace-throwing incident, Heffer disagreed, claiming that suspension was too severe. He began earnestly but his words were soon lost in uproar: 'You don't need a sledgehammer to . . .'

TORY BACK-BENCHER Jonathan Aitken has often been quoted for his quip a few years ago of Margaret Thatcher: 'I wouldn't say she was open-minded on the Middle East so much as empty-headed. For instance, she probably thinks that Sinai is the plural of sinuses.'

OF THE now defunct SDP, Labour MP George Foulkes said, 'It is the heterosexual wing of the Liberal Party.'

TORY BACK-BENCHER Robert Jones received loud applause at the Conservative Conference about a decade ago (before he was an MP) when he touched upon the disagreement of former premier Ted Heath towards the policies being pursued by Mrs Thatcher. 'Margaret Thatcher and Ted Heath both have a great vision,' he said. 'The difference is that Margaret Thatcher has a vision that Britain will one day be great again, and Ted Heath has a vision that Ted Heath one day will be great again.'

MP RICHARD PAGE tells of the occasion on which he was due to address a non-political gathering, as guest speaker, when the chairman of the meeting, an elderly ex-army officer type, expressed his dissatisfaction with politicians generally. He made a number of derogatory remarks about MPs, then called upon Mr Page to make his speech. The chairman could only wriggle in his seat, looking embarrassed and red-faced, as Mr Page opened his remarks with: 'I spoke a couple of days ago at the Annual General Meeting of the National Homosexuals' and Lesbians' Pacifist Association. I therefore apologize to you, Mr Chairman, for the fact that you will have heard my remarks before . . .'

NICHOLAS SOAMES, the MP for Crawley, is an affable and well-liked member who has, on occasions, caused much amusement by his insulting style. Labour MP Paul Boateng has an extremely trendy – some would say odd – taste in clothes. He regularly attends the House of Commons in loose-fitting baggy suits with wide shoulders. On one occasion, when he rose to address the House, the chamber was reduced to laughter by Nicholas Soames shouting, 'Would Sir like to return for another fitting?'

Some of Soames's worst insults have not been reported by the Press Gallery. When Nelson Mandela was due to visit London, the Shadow Leader of the House of Commons, Dr John Cunningham, asked, at business questions, if the Leader of the House, Sir Geoffrey Howe, would find 'proper accommodation for Mr Nelson Mandela to address members when he comes here next week?' As Sir Geoffrey rose to his feet, Nicholas Soames was heard to bellow: 'What about the rifle range?'

NOT MANY people outside the world of politics fully

understand the purpose of the Whips. All parties have them. These are MPs whose job is to secure the maximum possible attendance of their colleagues during a vote.

The Government Whips' aim is to ensure that government business is carried. Since 1983, the Conservative Party has had a healthy parliamentary majority and so the Whip's job has been somewhat easier. However, under the last Labour government, when they only had a majority of one, being a Whip was a thankless task.

Party Whips have various methods of persuading colleagues not only to wait for a late vote, but also to support their own side when the vote comes. Young MPs are sometimes enticed to be loyal with the hint that their absence at voting time may delay their chances of future promotion. Some Whips are less subtle, particularly when they are dealing with an older backbencher, who is unlikely to fall for the loss-of-promotion line.

A number of years ago it used to be the practice of the government to station a Whip at each exit of the House during the early part of the evening. The Whips would then stop all their own party's MPs as they were leaving, telling them that they must remain until the later votes were concluded.

On one occasion the flamboyant Tory back-bencher Gerald Nabarro was in the process of leaving when he was stopped by a Whip who pointed out that there were still votes to come. 'It doesn't matter, I've had enough. I'm going,' Nabarro responded. He was surprised to receive the response 'OK, f**k off then.' On this occasion, the insulting behaviour worked. Nabarro stayed on for the late votes.

Such abuse does not always pay off and can backfire badly, particularly if the Whip does not know the man he is dealing with. Some years back, Walter Bromley-Davenport, a Tory MP, was a junior government Whip and he was trying to prevent Conservative MPs leaving before business had finished. He was waiting near one of the exits to the House of Commons when a young man whom he took to be a new MP approached him. 'Where are you going?' he inquired. 'I'm going home,' came the reply. 'No, you're not, you're staying for the next vote,' Bromley-Davenport responded. 'Why should I stay for the next vote?' the obstinate young man retorted. 'I'm going home.' At this, Bromley-Davenport lost his temper. 'You are staying here!' he shouted at the erring MP, and kicked the man in the seat of his pants. He was rather mortified to find that he had just been 'addressing' the Belgian Ambassador. His career in the Whip's office ended the next day!

Such a difficulty would never happen to the Tory MP and senior government Whip, Sydney Chapman, who is far too courteous to treat anyone in such a fashion. He is actually polite to the point of chivalry, even when chasing after missing MPs. He once had to telephone a number of backbenchers to ask them to return to the House of Commons for an unexpected late vote. Upon telephoning one particular colleague, he was informed by a female voice at the other end of the phone that the MP was not at home but was expected shortly. Mr Chapman gave his name, said that he was a colleague of the MP, and that he wanted to speak to him. He mentioned that he could be contacted in the Whips' office, and then awaited the return call. The MP never telephoned back, nor did he appear at the vote, despite Mr Chapman's very clear instructions.

On seeing the missing MP in the House the next day, Mr Chapman inquired why he had not returned the call and why he had not voted. 'Oh, was it you?' the MP said. 'When I got home the au pair said that she had a phone call from a very strange man and that when he had started talking about whipping, she just put down the phone.'

However, the long hours of work in the Whips office sometimes even take their toll on someone as polite as Mr Chapman. On one occasion at the House, a long-winded MP was boring colleagues with his expertise on the tactics of the IRA in Northern Ireland. The MP, a self-styled expert, after a long and boring explanation of why the IRA bombers behave in a particular way, referred to a recent bombing attack and said 'They actually meant to bomb M&S but instead hit B&Q.' Rising to leave, Sydney Chapman ended the discussion with the barb 'perhaps the bombers were dyslexic.'

ALTHOUGH THE House of Commons rarely rises before ten in the evening, the Press Gallery is usually empty by tea-time. The Conservative Party Chairman, Chris Patten, underlined this when he told MPs, while glancing at an empty Press Gallery: 'Sometimes, if you want to keep a secret, announce it in the House of Commons.'

THE CONSERVATIVE MP Geoffrey Dickens is fond of telling a story – which he insists is true – about how he once inadvertently insulted one of his constituents.

He relates how at a summer fête he was asked to open, a very ugly woman asked for an autograph. 'Certainly – if you would care to drop me a note at the House of Commons, I will be delighted to send you a photograph,' he volunteered. About a month later, a charming letter arrived from the woman and after her signature she had bravely written 'Horseface' in brackets. Mr Dickens, filled with admiration for the way in which she had come to terms with her repulsive looks, decided to enter into the spirit of things. With a felt-tip pen he wrote across his photograph: 'To my dear friend Horseface – love and best wishes, Geoffrey Dickens.'

After the photo was duly posted, Mr Dickens happened to speak to his secretary – who informed him that she had written 'Horseface' after the woman's name on the letter, in case he had forgotten the lady in question.

JOHN BIFFEN, commenting on the views of Michael Heseltine: 'They are from the Henley School of Socialism.'

MP TIM DEVLIN, the youngest Tory in the House, did not have a high regard for at least one of his own party's former Whips about whom he said: 'He is of limited intelligence and does not have an original idea in his head. He is like one of Pavlov's dogs.'

DURING THE committee stage of the Football Spectators' Bill, Conservative MPs were becoming extremely weary with hearing patronizing speeches from the Labour side on the subject of soccer. After a tirade from Labour's Joe Ashton, which appeared to suggest that only Socialists knew about the game, Tory MP Steve Norris, exasperated, rose to his feet to debunk what he had just heard:

'He was clearly intent on presenting a picture of a Hovis-advertisement world in which people put on their cloth caps, put their pigeons in the loft, let out the ferret, got out the whippet, went down to the pub, had a couple of pints, wobbled back home on the bike to the sounds of Dvořák as the New World Symphony rippled through the clogs cracking on to the cobbled pavement, kicked the wife, battered the cat, and went off to see Bolton take on Preston as if it were a gradely world where men were men and women were there to make the tea when the men got home.' It was a tremendous performance, and proof, if any were needed, that properly applied sarcasm can be devastating.

SOMEONE RECENTLY remarked that Labour MP Austin Mitchell takes a 'keen interest in minority interest groups. But then he would have to – he works for Sky-TV.' Be that as it may, Mr Mitchell is always worth listening to in the House and is never reticent in passing his opinion, even on his own colleagues:

Of his party's former leader, Jim Callaghan, he has said: 'As Moses, he would have mistimed his arrival at the parting of the waves.'

At one time, unhappy with the management of his party, Mr Mitchell mocked: 'I don't belong to any organized party – I'm Labour.'

And, about the same time, commenting on his own party's policies: 'Recirculated sewage is still sewage.'

On former Industry Minister Douglas Hogg's assertion that the steel industry in Britain had a bright future, he said: 'A declaration of confidence from the government in their present state is more a kiss of death than an endorsement.'

DOUGLAS HOGG, the son of Lord Hailsham, is regarded by many as a 'chip off the old block'. In a very short space of time, he has not only established himself as an excellent minister, being fully in command of his brief, but also as someone who relishes a good insult. During an argument with one of the Tory 'knights of the shires' he bellowed: 'The Tory Party may have made you a knight, but it has not made you a gentleman.'

When he was questioned by the burly Scottish Labour MP, Tommy Graham, on the future of the Scottish steel industry, Mr Hogg, looking at Mr Graham's girth, retorted, 'My advice to him is that he should not lead with his chins but reflect more carefully before he asks questions.'

Recently, it has almost seemed that at question time in the House, he spends more time trading insults than he does giving parliamentary answers. A few months ago, at one question time alone, he managed to assail four Labour MPs in a little over five minutes. To Labour's Shadow spokesman Gordon Brown, he said, 'There are a number of unpleasant features about the honourable gentleman. He should be profoundly ashamed.' To the Deputy Shadow Leader of the House, Bruce Grocott, he said, 'That is the sort of dreary question that we have got used to hearing from Labour members.' To back-bench MP, Dale Campbell-Savours, he retorted, brushing aside the original question, 'Rampant inflation and massive taxation. That is the policy of the Labour Party and we are going to remind the electorate until they are fed up with it,' which prompted Mr Campbell-Savours to shout, 'What drug is he on?'

However, he provoked perhaps a stronger response than he expected when he said to MP George Foulkes, 'This whinging and whining is amusing and pathetic.' This prompted Mr Foulkes to shout back, 'This arrogant little shit hasn't answered one question.'

Trading insults in the House of Commons is one thing, but using four-letter words is another. The most taboo four-letter word of all is, of course, 'liar'. Mr Foulkes did not go this far, but nevertheless what he had said prompted the Speaker to ask him to withdraw '*that* word immediately'. Mr Foulkes got a second bite of the cherry with his reply: 'Which word do you want me to withdraw? Little? Arrogant? Or shit?' 'You know the word,' said the Speaker, and Mr Foulkes then obliged.

THE VIEW of Tory MP Teddy Taylor on the European Community does not seem to leave any room for argument. He has said, 'It is a most profligate, wasteful and useless organization.'

LORD DONOUGHUE, who as Bernard Donoughue was an assistant to Jim Callaghan, has not been afraid to insult his former colleagues. When asked his view on members of the TUC General Council during the late 1970s (the period which encompassed the 'Winter of Discontent' and the downfall of the last Labour government) he said, of the whole Council, 'If it had been constituted of personal representatives of Mrs Thatcher, it could not have acted more effectively in the Conservative leader's interest.'

FIERY AND outspoken, Labour MP Clare Short is not afraid to voice an opinion, not even on her own leader Neil Kinnock: 'Playing the big tough leader and kicking everyone around is the mistake he's been making. He needs to go back to the kind of politics he used to represent and to the personal style of being more open and respectful of other people.'

DURING A DEBATE on aid to Africa, the government's case was being presented to the Commons by Foreign Office Minister, Mark Lennox-Boyd, who was standing in during the absence of the Minister for Overseas Aid, Lynda Chalker, who was not in Britain at the time. Mr Lennox-Boyd did quite well, even though this was not strictly his subject, but after he had completed his speech, former Liberal leader, Sir David Steel cracked: 'The Minister was good enough to tell the House that he was not an expert on this subject and then went on to prove it . . .'

AUTHOR AND back-bench Tory MP Julian Critchley is always worth listening to in debate. His speeches positively crackle with wit and usually contain more than a hint of insult. In a debate on the Press, he ventured: 'The British tabloid newspaper is as British as the football hooligan – and just as welcome.'

When he was faced with an argument which he did not really think much of from the then Tory MP Peter Bruinvels, he responded, 'My honourable friend is beyond satire.'

During a Budget debate he pointed out that every fourth year, just before a general election, the nation was faced with a tax-cutting budget. In the intervening years, taxes were frequently raised again. This led him to conclude sarcastically that there was 'great merit in having a general election every year'. His barbs are sometimes rather too acerbic for his own good. In the same debate he said, 'As a back-bencher of very long standing, I can remember the time when Margaret Thatcher was a brunette.'

And in 1980 he caused an uproar by anonymously penning the following on the then Prime Minister: 'She is didactic, tart and obstinate. The first year of her government was set to martial music; brass, over which her shrill contralto could be heard urging friend and foe to go over the top. There is a quality to that gritty voice which, when combined with a fierce and unrelenting glare, and the repetition of the obvious, amounts to the infliction of pain.'

Of his friend Michael Heseltine, he is rather kinder, calling him 'a rabble-rouser to the gentry'.

ENOCH POWELL has said of former Tory premier Ted

Heath: 'He executed somersaults with the unselfconsciousness of the professional civil servant. After all, we keep civil servants to perform somersaults – that is what they are selected and trained to do. But although events sometimes overturn politicians, it is a rather appalling spectacle when a politician with apparent unselfconsciousness can do the precise opposite to that which he had previously advocated and stood for.'

LABOUR MP Dennis Canavan usually sits on the 'bovver boys' bench'* with Labour left-winger Dennis Skinner. He is frequently insulting – and amusing.

On 2 November 1983, during the course of a speech in which he assailed the Conservative MP Michael Forsyth, he said '. . . the honourable member for Stirling is two-faced when he says that delay in the sale of council houses is not permissible.' An allegation that an honourable member is two-faced is, of course, unparliamentary and the gibe led to an interruption from the Deputy Speaker, who told Mr Canavan in no uncertain terms that the remark was not acceptable and he expected it to be withdrawn.

Unabashed, Mr Canavan retorted that he had 'got away with it many times before'. At this apparent challenging of his ruling, the Deputy Speaker became impatient and firmly told the Labour MP that, irrespective of what had been allowed previously, he expected the offending remark to be withdrawn.

At last, it appeared that Mr Canavan was willing to back down as he started, 'As it is you who make the request, Mr Deputy Speaker, I will rephrase my comment . . .'

And, continuing perfectly within the rules of order,

* This is the front bench, below the gangway, on the Opposition side of the House.

Canavan said, 'Janus was a godlike figure in Roman mythology who had two faces – one facing one way and one facing the other. The honourable member for Stirling, who is my Member of Parliament, has some similarities to Janus.'

WHEN REFERRING to each other in the House of Commons, MPs are not permitted to call each other by name, but need to refer to the constituency of the MP concerned. During a rather heated debate, the Labour MP for Holborn and St Pancras, Mr Frank Dobson, made a number of remarks to which the Tory MP for Perth and Kinross, Mr Nicholas Fairbairn, objected strongly. During the course of his rebuttal of Mr Dobson's remarks, Mr Fairbairn added insult to injury by referring to Dobson as 'the MP for the two tube stations'.

It is always a rather dangerous pastime to cross swords with this former Scottish Law Officer. Rather like dancing on thin ice, one is always at risk. During a debate on the proposal to add fluoride to Britain's water supplies, Mr Fairbairn achieved the near impossible by stopping Edwina Currie in her tracks. He was arguing against fluoridation and said, 'Fluoride is a potent catalase poison which is cumulative. Nobody on any side of the argument denies that it is toxic.'

At this point, Mrs Currie intervened and expressed her disagreement: 'Fluoridation has been nothing but good.' And unwisely she added: 'Anything is a poison if we take enough of it. Were we to spread-eagle my honourable friend on the floor of the House and pour absolutely pure H_2O into him, it would kill him – or anyone else subjected to that treatment – in hours.' Mr Fairbairn, face expressionless, responded devastatingly, 'All the poison that my honourable friend suggested I would happily take, rather than be spread-eagled on the floor of the House by her.'

When asked for his view, on most things he replies with a generous lacing of vitriol. Of former Prime Minister Edward Heath: 'He has no place in the Party. He has no future in Parliament. He has no place, for Parliament is a generous place; democracy is a generous thing. May I suggest he pursues his alternative career and conducts orchestras, since he does not know how to conduct himself.'

Challenged by Labour MP Dennis Canavan during a long debate to 'make his learned opinion available', Mr Fairbairn silenced him with the retort: 'Only if the honourable gentleman would forgo his ignorant ones.'

THE LATE Ian Gow, was, in all respects, an honourable man. His brutal murder by the IRA not only robbed parliament of a talented member, but has deprived many of us of a cherished and loyal friend.

When speaking in debate, he was invariably courteous and polite except on two subjects, when he could always be called upon to be less than complimentary. On the Liberal party, he never missed an opportunity to berate them for their lack of attendance during debates. The other subject upon which Ian would wax insulting would be on the subject of Mr Edward Heath. Should Mr Heath's name enter the debate, Ian Gow could always be relied upon for a sarcastic gibe or barbed insult against the former leader of his party. In a debate on exports, only a few weeks before he was killed, he said: 'Unaccountably, my right honourable friend (Mr Heath) is not in his place. No doubt he is conducting an orchestra in a distant land – I suppose that he is contributing to exports. I think that some of my honourable friends would like to export him – but who would purchase him?'

On an earlier occasion, during a debate on the Channel Tunnel, Ian Gow suggested that a Committee be established to consider some of the more boring aspects of the Channel Tunnel project. He then went on to suggest that former Prime Minister Edward Heath should be a member of the Committee. As he warmed to the subject, he corrected himself and said that he thought he should be 'the only member of the Committee' causing much amusement on the Conservative benches. The amusement turned to loud laughter when Gow then changed his mind, saying that perhaps, after all, Heath should not be on the Channel Tunnel Committee. Recalling the Heath Government's change of policies shortly after being elected, Gow endorsed the suggestion that, with Heath in charge, the Channel Tunnel might 'start at Dover, get halfway across the Channel and then do a U-turn and come back.'

DURING THE long Commons committee stage of the NHS and Community Care Bill, John Maxton, a member of Labour's front-bench Scottish team, was referring to the range of operations currently available at hospitals, which he feared would be under threat from the government's proposals. He referred to a particular hospital, and to a vasectomy operation that he had undergone there: 'Would this operation be at risk?' he inquired. He was silenced by the barb from Tory Jerry Hayes who shouted back: 'I didn't know that hospital did micro-surgery!'

STILL DURING the committee stage of the NHS and Community Care Bill, Welsh Labour MP Alun Michael spoke at length on a matter which could have been disposed of in a few minutes. The subject was the future availability of drugs, which he did rather labour somewhat. This caused fellow Welsh MP, Tory Nicholas Bennett, to muse, much to Labour's annoyance, that he hoped there 'would soon be drugs available to cure verbal diarrhoea'.

It was also in that committee that Bennett referred to Alice Mahon, the MP for Halifax, as 'The Madame Defarge of the Labour Party'.

Nick Bennett has, since his election to the House in 1987, become something of a *bête noire* for a number of opposition MPs. Commenting on the collapse in the polls of the Liberal Democrats in 1989 he said: 'Electoral support for the Liberal Democrats would be impressive only if it was measured on the Richter scale.'

When it was announced, during the summer of 1990, that Tory back-bencher Michael Latham (Melton) was to give up politics for the Church, Mr Bennett commented: 'If you become a grocer I suppose you get groceries for nothing; if you become a doctor, you get well for nothing, if you become a politician, you speak for nothing, but if you become a preacher, you get good for nothing.'

At a meeting, when a heckler interrupted him with a cry of 'Rubbish', he responded with, 'I'll discuss your arguments later.'

To another heckler who continually interrupted him Mr Bennett remarked, 'You'd better shut up, or else.' This led to the retort: 'Or else what?' At which point the MP dispatched him with: 'Or else you will leave this meeting as ignorant as when you came in.'

To an interruption from a Socialist he once retorted: 'It is a pity your brain has become disconnected from your mouth.'

OUR HONOURABLE friends across the Atlantic have their share of hard-hitting orators too. I can think of quite a few MPs to whom one could apply Canadian

Larry Zolf's remark about Joe Clark: 'No shirt is too young to be stuffed.'

AMERICAN PRESIDENT Harry S Truman once said: 'I never give them hell. I just tell the truth, and they think it is hell.'

Speaking of the United States Senate, he said, 'During the first six months I was there, I wondered how I had made it – later I wondered how the rest of them made it.'

He said of his record in office, 'I was about as popular as a skunk in the parlour,' and, displaying more than a little cynicism, 'if you can't convince them, confuse them.'

'Some of the Presidents were great and some of them weren't. I can say that, because I wasn't one of the great Presidents, but I had a good time trying to be one.'

Truman did not have a very high opinion of some of those who follow religion. He once remarked, 'I think there is an immense shortage of Christian charity among so-called Christians.'

He said of Eisenhower, 'He just sat on his ass when Castro came to power and acted like he didn't notice what was going on. Of course, the Russians didn't sit on their asses, and they got him lined up on their side, which is what you have to expect if you've got a god-damn-fool in the White House.'

On critic Paul Hume: 'An eight-ulcer man on a four-ulcer job . . . a guttersnipe is a gentleman compared to him.'

Truman once bitingly said about American journalist Drew Pearson, (who wanted General Vaughan to be dismissed): 'No-son-of-a-bitch like Pearson is going to prevail on me to discharge anyone by some smart-alec statement over the air.'

And his view of General MacArthur: 'I fired him

because he wouldn't respect the authority of the President. I didn't fire him because he was a dumb son of a bitch, although he was, but that's not against the law for generals. If it was, half to three-quarters of them would be in jail.'

PRESIDENTIAL CANDIDATE Adlai Stevenson could, in public, be bruising with his invective. However, unlike Ronald Reagan, he was near to useless on television and consequently not a success with the American electorate. Among Stevenson's many gibes, the following are the most memorable:

'A politician is a statesman who approaches every question with an open mouth.'

On tabloid newspaper editors: 'An editor is one who separates the wheat from the chaff and prints the chaff.'

On the Republican Party's policies: 'Nobody can stand for election on a bushel of eels.'

On being disparagingly referred to as 'an intellectual' he cracked: 'Eggheads unite – you have nothing to lose but your yokes.' This led to the retort from one of Stevenson's opponents: 'When eggheads try to be funny, the yolk usually breaks.'

Criticizing the Republicans: 'If they stop telling lies about me, I will stop telling the truth about them.'

When General Eisenhower entered politics as his opponent, he said: 'It is a tragedy that the Old Guard has succeeded in doing what Hitler's best generals never could do: they captured Eisenhower.' And, again on Ike, 'He is a me-too candidate running on a yes-but platform by a has-been staff.' As Eisenhower became more popular with the electorate, Stevenson's barbs became more bitter: 'Eisenhower is worried about my funny bone – and I am worried about his backbone.'

To which shortly afterwards, President Eisenhower

responded: 'Adlai Stevenson's no rail-splitter – just a hair-splitter.'

Of President Richard Nixon Stevenson said: 'He's the kind of politician who could cut down a tree and then mount the stump and make a speech for conservation.'

'An Independent is the guy who wants to take politics out of politics.'

'He who slings mud generally loses ground.'

'Man does not live by words alone, despite the fact that sometimes he has to eat them.'

Criticizing the voters he said: 'I sometimes marvel at the extraordinary docility with which Americans submit to speeches.'

PRESIDENT EISENHOWER did not agree with the suggestion that the voters were lacking in intelligence: 'It is only governments that are stupid, not the masses of people.'

And, criticizing his failed opponent Adlai Stevenson: 'An intellectual is a man who takes more words than necessary to tell more than he knows.'

AMERICAN REPUBLICAN politician Barry Goldwater did not have much respect for Democrat President Johnson, of whom he said 'He fiddled while Detroit burned and he faddled while men died.'

AMERICAN SENATOR Hugh Scott said after the Watergate scandal: 'The transcripts revealed deplorable, disgusting, shabby and immoral performance by everyone involved, not excluding President Nixon.'

RICHARD NIXON'S vice-president, Spiro Agnew,

launched a vitriolic attack on the leaders of Eastern Europe in the days before *glasnost*. During a speech in New Orleans, he said the leaders of Eastern Europe were 'ideological eunuchs, whose most comfortable position is straddling the fence'.

AMERICAN SECRETARY of State, Dean Rusk, clearly did not trust Russian Premier Khrushchev: 'He may have been an affable grandfather at 70 – but at 68 he put missiles in Cuba. We don't believe anyone reforms between 68 and 70.'

SENATOR NORRIS COTTON liked a good insult. He once said of the US Senate: 'They are in such a mood that if someone introduced the Ten Commandments, they'd cut them down to eight.'

When asked to comment on his colleagues, he expressed the view that 'There are a lot of grindstones in politics in need of noses.'

And he also was not afraid to insult former Russian leader Khrushchev, with the quote from Emerson: 'The louder he talked of his honour, the faster we counted our spoons.'

LYNDON B JOHNSON, President of the United States from 1963 to 1968, raised more than a few eyebrows with his response to the inquiry as to why he had appointed a dissenter to his administration. The then President said bluntly that he would 'rather have him inside the tent pissing out, than outside pissing in'.

Johnson seems to have been fond of using references to urine in his insults. He once said of the Association of American States: 'They couldn't pour piss out of a shoe if the instructions were written on the heel.'

On his political opponents: 'They've been peddling eyewash about themselves and hogwash about the Democrats. What they need is a good mouthwash.'

And, on an opponent: 'Never trust a man whose eyes are too close to his nose.'

Among his other cracks, the most memorable are:

'When you crawl out on a limb, you always have to find another one to crawl back on.'

'A town that cannot support one lawyer can always support two.'

Speaking about the American's attitude to taxes: 'The nation which had fought a revolution against taxation without representation discovered that some of its citizens weren't much happier about taxation with representation.'

Continuing his line in effective but coarse insults, Johnson said of Gerald Ford: 'He is so dumb that he can't fart and chew gum at the same time.'

AFTER HE left office, former American Secretary of State Henry Kissinger said, with more than a degree of accuracy, 'Now when I bore people at a party, they think it's their fault.'

His views on those he had served: 'If you've seen one President, you've seen them all.'

EDWARD KOCH, former Mayor of New York, is known for his controversial and insulting manner. He euphemistically describes this as a 'willingness to speak out'. This 'willingness' has over the years been castigated by friend and foe alike who think he has too often been insulting in his remarks. Mr Koch himself admits that this is a weakness. Happily, for connoisseurs of the insult, it appears he has not decided to modify his behaviour.

162

To a particularly rude female constituent who also exhibited in her letters traits of anti-Semitism, he replied, after he had received half a dozen or so letters: 'I received your last six letters and I have placed them in the loony bin where they belong.' After receiving a few further replies from Koch in a similar vein, she stopped writing.

Somehow, I do not think Mayor Koch's insulting approach will catch on in Britain. Most MPs receive crank mail and, to my knowledge, if they reply at all they send a soothing response. Should a British politician answer a constituent in the manner of Mr Koch, it is certain that the contents of the reply would soon be blazoned across the local newspaper 'proving', his opponents would say, 'that he is unfit to hold office'.

However, during his three terms of office as Mayor of New York, Ed Koch seems to have got away with more insults than many other politicians could successfully manage in a lifetime. On Joseph V Reed, former Under Secretary for Political and General Assembly Affairs at the UN: 'Rather unctuous and silly. He isn't a diplomat, he's a dope.' Ed Koch, however, is not the only person who has a low opinion of Mr Reed. Former Senator Thomas Eagleton once said of Reed, 'He is a fourteen-carat nitwit.'

Of the United Nations itself, for which New York is the host city: he has said, 'It's a cesspool.'

Whether you like him or not, you have to admire Koch, for he is afraid of no one. Commenting on some religious leaders he has been positively vitriolic. Of Minister Louis Farrakhan of the National Church of Islam he has said 'He is a charismatic figure and a superb speaker. So was Adolf Hitler. And like Hitler, Farrakhan is a hatemonger. When he preaches, truth is abandoned.'

Of Father Lawrence Lucas of the Roman Catholic Church in Manhattan: 'He is a theological maverick in clerical garb. He has given new meaning to the word vile.'

Of his own city's bishop, Paul Moore, he said: 'He is more a Pontius Pilate than a humble worker at the feet of the poor.'

When he had been 'savaged' in the New York newspapers, he gave this view: 'Never trust a smiling reporter.'

But he reserved much of his venom for journalist Jack Newfield, about whom he said, 'He shows up at all the right parties, uses his column to curry favour with all of the right people, but has a little problem: he's a self-admitted liar. His style could be characterized as misstatement, omission and sleight of hand. For him, truth is putty, to be twisted and squeezed into one fantastic shape or another. The result is an ugly self-portrait of the artist as a bitter man.'

By comparison his comments on the official Soviet news agency sound rather like praise: 'It's always a compliment to be denounced by Tass.'

Although Ed Koch is a Democrat, he is not afraid to speak his mind on other members of his own party. On Presidential candidate Jesse Jackson he has said: 'As a person, there is much to admire in him. As a potential President of the United States, there is much to fear. He is far to the left and while many of his domestic proposals are laudable, they could bankrupt America. Jews and other supporters of Israel would have to be crazy to vote for him.'

On troubled American financier Donald Trump: 'Trump likes to make a big deal about the big deals he makes. I agree with the man who said, "I wouldn't believe him even if his tongue were notarized." For the most part he strikes me as a miserable person.'

Despite the years of invective, however, Koch was careful not to alienate his own electors. Mayoral candidate Bernard Epton, who was standing for office in

Chicago, was clearly not as subtle. He said of his voters, 'They are just slime.' He lost the election.

RONALD REAGAN has been one of the most success-ful Presidents of the United States and yet, in England at any rate, he is regarded by many as a second-rate film actor who was rather lucky to be elected to the most powerful office in the world. Those who have met Ronald Reagan, who have heard him on the platform or who have studied his career, do not share this view. Indeed, every opponent of Ronald Reagan has made the mistake of underestimating him. Although not an intellectual, he is certainly a shrewd political operator who on occasions effectively uses self-deprecation to win over an audience.

He is not afraid, of course, of using a barbed insult against his opponents, but he will sometimes, for effect, gently insult himself, but with a style that few have managed to match. I heard him speak at Guildhall in London in 1989 giving his first major speech since leav-ing office. It was a masterly performance delivered with-out a teleprompter and with hardly a reference to a note, causing Michael Heseltine, who was sitting in front of me (and who is himself one of our best political orators) to remark, 'A tremendous performance.'

Reagan told a story against himself, relating to an incident that occurred when he was the Governor of California. At that time, he was asked by President Nixon to represent him at a gathering and to address a group in Mexico City. After Reagan finished his speech, he sat down to rather half-hearted, unenthusi-astic applause. He was, he said, quite embarrassed. His embarrassment increased when the speaker who fol-lowed him, speaking in Spanish – which Reagan did not understand – was applauded at every paragraph. To hide his embarrassment, Reagan started clapping

Ronald Reagan
and the
Magic Baseball Bat.

before everyone else and longer than anyone else until the American Ambassador leaned over to him to say, 'I wouldn't do that if I were you – he's interpreting your speech.'

At an election rally, insulting himself: 'You know when you're getting old. When you're faced with two temptations and you choose the one that gets you home by 9pm.'

In a similar vein: 'I am thinking of donating my body to science. But they have taken so much away from me over the years that I'll be sent to the lab in a Jiffy bag!'

When asked for his autograph by a fan on a picture showing him with a chimpanzee from the film *Bedtime for Bonzo*: 'I am the one with the watch.'

Commenting on the Democratic Party's programme during the 1988 election: 'They have made inflated claims about what they intend to do. But that's only to be expected. After all, they are the party of inflation.'

'A hippy is someone who looks like Tarzan, walks like Jane and smells like Cheeta.'

Commenting on Vietnam war protestors: 'Their signs said "Make love not war." It didn't look to me as if they were capable of either.'

When meeting the space shuttle astronauts: 'I just got back from outer space too . . . Capitol Hill.'

On Libya: 'We are not going to tolerate these attacks from states run by the strangest collection of misfits, loony tunes, and squalid criminals since the advent of the Third Reich.'

His effective swipe at Colonel Gaddafi was: 'Not only a barbarian, but flaky.'

Insulting his opponent in the 1980 Presidential election: 'Depression is when you are out of work. A recession is when your neighbour is out of work, and a recovery is when Jimmy Carter is out of work.'

'Politics is the second oldest profession. It bears a very close resemblance to the first.'

'The Kremlin is like a baby – it has an appetite at one end and no sense of responsibility at the other.'

One of Ronald Reagan's favourite insulting stories is about a Russian who was boasting that he had read many books and claimed that Communists were better read than capitalists. 'After all,' the Russian argued, 'every Communist has read the works of Marx and Lenin.' 'Yes,' the American replied. 'I accept that a Communist is someone who has read the works of Marx and Lenin. However, a capitalist is someone who understands the works of Marx and Lenin.'

When he was Governor of California, and was concerned by what his local state legislature had done to a proposal he had made, he commented: 'I have wondered at times what the Ten Commandments would have looked like if Moses had had to run them through a state legislature.'

On his initial reluctance to run for office: 'I almost became neither a hawk nor a dove, but a chicken.'

Turning an insult around, when he was Governor of California, Reagan responded to the taunt of 'pig' shouted by a heckler in the audience: 'I am very proud to be called a pig. It stands for pride, integrity, and guts.'

And his view of government: 'Governments tend not to solve problems, only to rearrange them.'

On left-wingers in America: 'The leaders of the Democratic Party have gone so far left, they've left America.'

'I've spoken in Britain many times over the years and my Conservative speeches never needed any translation – except perhaps at times for the Labour Party.'

American Congresswoman Pat Schroeder said quite accurately of President Reagan: 'He has achieved a breakthrough in political technology – the Teflon-coated Presidency. He sees to it that nothing sticks to him.'

GEORGE BUSH, elected President of the United States in 1988, had a nice line during his election campaign: 'My opponent has a problem. He won't get elected unless things get worse – and things won't get worse unless he gets elected.'

BARRY GOLDWATER, the American Republican politician and one-time contender for the Presidency, warned: 'A government that is big enough to give you all you want, is big enough to take it all away.'

3
'All Politics is Apple Sauce'

THE US Senator Chauncey Depew, who thought of himself as a good speech-maker, received the following insult from Joseph Choat: 'Mr Depew says that if you open my mouth and drop in a dinner, up will come a speech. But I warn you, that if you open your mouths and drop in one of Mr Depew's speeches, up will come your dinners.'

STANLEY BALDWIN, once infuriated because he was not called by the Speaker, referred to the Speaker's eye as 'that most elusive organ that nature has ever yet created'.

IT WAS Lady Violet Bonham Carter who remarked: 'Tories are always wrong, but they are always wrong at the right moment.'

INSULTS AGAINST the BBC have been around as long as the Corporation itself. Back-bencher Brendan Bracken, in a debate on the BBC, remarked: 'It is true that a joke in the BBC's mouth is no laughing matter.'

ONCE, WHEN Herbert Morrison was rambling on from the Labour front bench, he made some reference to the poor attendance in the chamber, causing a back-bencher, Kenneth Pickthorne, to remark, 'It ill becomes those few of us who are boring the rest of us to complain about those who have stayed away.'

A BACK-BENCHER in 1940, commenting on the co-operation between Emmanuel Shinwell and Lord Winterton, which was regarded as highly unusual: 'They are like arsenic and old lace.'

A RUSSIAN comment on American military policy: 'The Pentagon has five sides on every issue.'

FRANCIS PYM, when Leader of the House of Commons, said of the now-defunct SDP: 'Stale claret in new bottles – it is a confidence trick not to be mistaken for the elixir of life.'

A TORY MP commenting on a speech by Labour member Denzil Davies: 'He is suffering from bottle fatigue.'

WHILE SHE was an MP, Mrs Sally Oppenheim was, for a time, the Conservative spokesman on prices. During a speech attacking Roy Hattersley, who was the minister responsible, she made a reference to 'the shop floor'. This prompted a cry from a Labour back-bencher that the only shop floor she knew anything about was that of Fortnum and Mason.

IN 1945, the Conservatives lost the General Election and Winston Churchill found himself no longer in office. In the Commons, there was a tremendous change of scene with many 'working class' Labour MPs taking their seats for the first time. An old Tory MP, surveying the new Labour members sitting in the chamber, was overheard to say: 'Who the hell are these people? They look like a load of damned constituents.'

LORD WYATT on Arthur Scargill: 'He appears in the tradition of Hereward the Wake, fighting on against the Normans though all can see the cause is hopeless.'

IN 1984 Senator Gary Hart said of former Vice-President Walter Mondale: 'He is mush. He's weak and his managers know it and they are scared.'

DURING THE Watergate hearings, Senator Sam Ervin described the Nixon administration's attempt to have the hearings in camera as 'executive poppycock'.

NOT ALL insults take place in the Chamber of the House of Commons. On the ground floor of the Houses of Parliament are the showers, which are taken communally. A conversation was recently overheard between a Conservative MP and a Labour back-bencher from a mining constituency.

Conservative MP: 'At least we public schoolboys and you miners don't mind showering together.'

Labour MP: 'No, the only difference between us is that we daren't bend down for the soap.'

A COMMENT made by Nance Garner to then Vice-President Lyndon Johnson: 'The vice-presidency of America isn't worth a pitcher of warm spit.'

THE MP Tom Sackville was overheard to comment acidly on a Labour MP: 'He has the ideal face for radio.'

SENATOR HUBERT HUMPHREY of the USA, criticizing his own party's poor fund-raising efforts, said, 'Only the Democratic Party would hold a dinner at which the speakers nearly outnumber the audience.'

THE WIFE of American politician Claude Pepper once said: 'The mistake a lot of politicians make is forgetting they've been appointed, and thinking they've been anointed.'

A GOVERNOR of Virginia once wrote to a man called Patrick Henry demanding an apology because Mr Henry was alleged to have called him a 'bob-tail' politician. The Governor said: 'I wish to know if this is true, and if true, your meaning.' In one of the few exchanges where the constituent got the better of the elected politician, Mr Henry replied: 'Sir, I do not recollect having called you a bob-tail politician at any time, but I think it probable that I have. Not recollecting the time or occasion, I cannot say what I meant, but if you will tell me what you think I meant, I will say whether you are correct. Yours sincerely . . .'

AMERICAN SENATOR Homer Fergusson said of a political opponent: 'An egghead . . . one who stands firmly on both feet in mid-air on both sides of an issue.'

WHEN SENATOR Bob Dole was asked whether he thought President Gorbachev of Russia had domestic problems in the USSR, he replied: 'I don't know about that, but when he last visited the States, we had to force him to catch the plane home.'

In 1990, when he was asked whom he thought the Democrats would choose to contest the next Presidential election against George Bush, Bob Dole replied: 'They're so short of candidates I hear they've asked President Gorbachev to run as a Democrat.'

PEER LORD BROUGHAM took a swipe at his learned friends when he said: 'A lawyer is someone who rescues your estate from your enemies and keeps it for himself.'

LEVI ESHKOL, a former Prime Minister of Israel, said of his own country's political propensities: 'Put three Zionists in a room – and they will form four political parties.'

SENATOR ALEXANDER WILEY has said: 'Dealing with Russia is like handling a jackass. You can talk to him and talk to him, but watch out he don't kick you.'

WHEN ASKED by the Press why he was standing for the American Senate as well as running for the post of Vice-President in the 1988 elections, Texan Democrat Lloyd Bentsen said, self-deprecatingly, that his decision reminded him of the vet who went into business with a taxidermist and used the slogan: 'Either way you get the dog back.'

SENATOR TED STEVENS, on himself: 'I'm a blunt bastard.'

LORD SAMUEL once said that the Civil Service had 'a difficulty for every solution'.

AMERICAN FRANK HOWLEY said crushingly of Khrushchev's threats: 'No pig-eyed bag of wind is going to push us out of Berlin.'

ALTHOUGH NOWADAYS he seems to be usually on the receiving end, during his period of office President Nixon was not short of insults to dish out. He once silenced a heckler with: 'The jaw-bone of an ass is just as dangerous a weapon today as it was in Samson's time.'

AT A party, Congressman Thomas O'Neill toasted Senator Dodd: 'Here's to the second nastiest drunk in town.'

IT IS unwise to brag in front of any Member of Parliament as most MPs have a ready line in insults, developed over the years by the necessity of having to address hostile audiences. When a rather pompous and smug businessman rambled on for far too long about the benefits of owning a Mercedes Benz car, he concluded his remarks by saying: 'All really famous people own a Mercedes – it is their favourite car.' He elicited the response from an MP: 'Well it was certainly Adolf Hitler's favourite.'

WHEN PARLIAMENT reassembled after the General Election in May 1979, Jim Callaghan, no longer Premier, found himself on the Opposition benches facing

Margaret Thatcher who had become Britain's first woman Prime Minister. He rose and with good grace said: 'Who would have thought that Britain would today have its first woman Prime Minister . . .' to which Tory Robert Atkins bellowed: 'As opposed to an old woman Prime Minister.' Which just goes to show that in politics there is no rule against kicking a man when he is down.

A P HERBERT, the former Independent MP said of the Tory Edward Boyle: 'Brilliant – but deplorable', and of Labour Arts minister Jennie Lee: 'A fallen angel, stopped by her own civil servants from doing what she wanted to do.'

JOHN F KENNEDY commented, at a dinner honouring a number of Nobel Prize winners: 'I think this is the most extraordinary collection of talent, of human knowledge, that has ever been gathered together at the White House – with the possible exception of when Thomas Jefferson dined alone.'

And, when asked why he did not hold a baby for an election photo: 'Kissing babies gives me asthma.'

His brother, Senator Robert Kennedy, said of the American public: 'One fifth of the people are against everyone all of the time.'

Robert Kennedy also showed that he did not have an entirely forgiving nature when it came to political insults. His favourite maxim was: 'Always forgive your enemies – but never forget their names.'

In a similar vein he remarked: 'Never complain, never explain. Get even.'

ONE MP said of Labour politician Herbert Morrison

that: 'The private papers he left behind were so dull and banal, they would only provide illumination if they were burned.'

IT WAS a Republican who referred to one of President Jimmy Carter's speeches as 'more mush from the wimp'.

HEADS OF STATE are fair game for insults. An Australian MP was overheard posing the question, 'What is over sixteen stone and still a lightweight?' The answer given was, 'David Lange, the Prime Minister of New Zealand.'

AFTER A forceful oration by Neil Kinnock, a Labour MP was overheard to say, 'He thinks bullshit baffles brains.'

TAKING A swipe at the Tories in 1989, Labour MP Tony Benn said: 'If capitalism depended on the intellectual quality of the Conservative party, it would end about lunchtime tomorrow.'

VICE-PRESIDENTIAL candidate Dan Quayle's television performance during the 1988 Presidential election campaign was described as being 'like Bambi on ice'.

LABOUR MP Ken Livingstone, commenting on colleague Gerald Kaufman: 'he has crawled so far up the backside of NATO that you can't see the soles of his feet.'

DURING A party on the Terrace of the House of Commons at about the time of the *Spycatcher* case, a Tory MP inquired: 'Have you heard the news? A demonstrator has just been arrested for causing a disturbance at the end of Downing Street. He was waving his fists and shouting "the government is insane". He'll probably be fined for being drunk.'

A Labour MP sarcastically retorted, 'No, he'll probably be given a twenty-year jail sentence for revealing a state secret!'

DESCRIPTION OF Lord Liverpool, the Tory statesman of the early nineteenth century, 'His lack of originality was such that, had he been present at the Creation, he would have begged God not to disturb chaos.'

A LIBERAL-DEMOCRAT jumble sale has been described as 'second-hand products being sold by third-rate politicians to bring forth money for a fifth-rate party'.

THE FORMER Governor of New York, Al Smith, said in response to an opponent's speech, 'However thin you slice it, it's still baloney.'

AFTER THE 1983 general election result was declared, one Labour politician was moved to remark that his own party's election manifesto was 'the longest suicide note in history'.

ON HEARING someone say that heavyweight Liberal MP Cyril Smith was 'an all-round talent' a fellow Liberal Democrat made the crack that the problem was 'it takes much too long to walk all round him'.

SEDENTARY SHOUT from a back-bencher, referring to Labour MP Gwyneth Dunwoody: 'She has all the charm and finesse of a sledge-hammer.'

TORY BACK-BENCHER Andrew Mitchell took a low swipe at the Liberal Democrats when, during a debate in the House, he stated: 'The popularity of the Liberal Party has sunk so low in the opinion polls that they are considering employing the services of Jacques Cousteau to see whether anything can be done to resuscitate it.'

AFTER A rather liberal speech by Labour Home Affairs spokesman, Barry Sheerman, Andrew Mitchell commented: 'I am amazed that he does not arrive at the Commons wearing a kipper tie, flared trousers and a pair of open-toed sandals. That would express the sentiments that he appears to hold.'

And, during a debate on local government, he lambasted the then Labour leader of Lambeth Council, Joan Twelves, for the poor service provided by that authority. Mr Mitchell acidly commented: 'Joan Twelves has refused to pay her community charge saying she will put the bill "in the bin". In Lambeth, it is extremely unlikely that the contents of the bin will be collected!'

ANONYMOUS COMMENT on Mayor LaGuardia of New York: 'Anyone who extends him the right hand of friendship is in danger of losing a couple of fingers'.

MR MICHAEL BROTHERTON was some years ago

Member of Parliament for Louth. Due to his apparent eagerness to give quotes to the Press on most subjects, he became known to some journalists as a 'rentaquote' MP. Some of his own colleagues however, started to refer to him as 'Louth the Mouth'.

MR PETER BOTTOMLEY commenting on Labour spokesman John Prescott: 'He just cannot keep his mouth shut.'

ANONYMOUS ON Neil Kinnock: 'In Kinnock Britain has at least produced a party leader worthy of assassination.'

A TORY remarked of the former Labour MP, Shirley Summerskill: 'She had a face like a well-kept grave.'
    Mrs Summerskill was not always on the receiving end. In the 1950s fellow Tory MPs Enoch Powell and Iain MacLeod had a habit of both popping up together to speak during the same debate. This led Mrs Summerskill to refer to them as 'Tweedledum and Tweedledee'.

COMMENT ON former Tory Cabinet minister Selwyn Lloyd: 'He could not tell the difference between pulling one's leg and breaking it.'

ONCE A tiresome MP berated his Whip for over fifteen minutes while expanding his views on some particular aspect of government policy. In an attempt to end the conversation, the Whip replied: 'Thank you very much – I'll make a mental note of that.' At which a passing back-bencher was heard to remark, 'On what?'

WHEN GEORGE BROWN said of the then Labour leader Michael Foot: 'The party should not be led by someone who has one eye and one leg', one of Foot's friends, referring to Brown's drinking habits, angrily snapped: 'In the country of the legless, the one-legged man is king.'

THE OPINION of American satirist Will Rogers was that: 'All politics is apple sauce.' And commenting on the American party system he said, 'The Republicans have their splits right after an election and Democrats have theirs just before.'

GEORGE ORWELL said of Clement Attlee: 'He reminds me of nothing so much as a dead fish before it has time to stiffen.'

COMMENT ON Kenneth Baker by Tory back-bencher: 'I don't think he has his hair cut, he just has an oil change.'

WHEN NEVILLE CHAMBERLAIN came back from Munich, the then Lord Cranborne was prompted to question, in a speech: 'Here is peace, but where is honour?'

WHEN ASKED if he thought Neil Kinnock was a 'silly ass', a left-wing Labour MP was heard to say: 'Kinnock is not silly.'

WHEN LABOUR MP Tony Blair was accused by a

journalist of being a 'yuppie Socialist', he replied that his public-school education was never a problem with working-class voters, 'only with middle-class journalists'.

AT AN election meeting, a particularly pompous colleague was asked what he had done in the Commons during the previous four years. He replied, 'I will have you know, sir, I have asked no fewer than ninety-seven parliamentary questions!' To which a heckler replied, 'Ignorant bastard!' Come polling day, he lost the seat.

4
Their Words Live On

THE VAST majority of insults are, of course, not anonymous – but not all are attributable. Some have been remembered while their originators have been forgotten, while others – such as poison-pen letters – have always been intended to be anonymous.

In the insults which follow, it has either not been possible to identify which politician is the abuser, or I have thought it wise not to record the names of the parties involved – for my own safety!

Here then are a number of insults which have been heard, and overheard, and for which credit must collectively go to elected representatives, on both sides of the Atlantic.

COMMENTING ON Labour's new policies, one MP said, 'Neil Kinnock deserves some credit for dragging his party into the 20th century, just in time for the rest of us to enter the 21st century. He also has proved that Lewis Carroll is alive and well and writing his speeches.'

QUOTE BY a contemporary on Lloyd George: 'He is a man of splendid abilities, but utterly corrupt. Like a rotten mackerel by moonlight, he shines and stinks.'

POLITICIANS DO not always get the best of hecklers. An MP rebuked a heckler with the comment: 'What if everyone was like you? It would be chaos. What if the whole country decided to run away from its problems?'

'Well,' the heckler responded, 'at least then we would all be running in the same direction.'

DURING THE early part of this century, when the Labour Party was in its infancy, it was described by a Liberal MP as 'a tick carried along on the asquithean sheep'.

IT WAS said of the MP George Lansbury by Conservatives that he 'let his bleeding heart run away with his bloody head and he lost his seat'.

WHEN ONE Minister, between the First and Second World Wars began a speech with the words, 'Well, Mr Speaker, I will try to compress what I have to say into an hour,' he was put off his stride with the shout, 'In that case, Mr Speaker, can we have the windows open?'

TWO YOUNG Conservatives from different wings of the party were overheard talking. The right-winger informed his colleague that his recent speech was very much like a river. At hearing this, the colleague was pleased. 'You mean it was a great outpouring of wisdom?'

'Not exactly,' the right-winger replied. 'I thought it was narrow at the head, broad at the mouth and completely wet.'

Heckler: 'I would rather vote for the devil than vote for you.'
Candidate: 'Yes, but your father is not standing.'

AFTER THE car accident at Chapaquiddick in which

a female passenger was drowned, it was said around Washington that the only person in the world now likely to accept a lift home from Edward Kennedy was Jacques Cousteau.

AN MP was irritated when he received the the bill for his son's school fees and these showed a huge increase. His irritation turned to anger when he noticed the account contained a spelling mistake and he was being asked 'to pay the sum of £5,000 per anum.'

He sent the bill back with a note stating that he 'would prefer to continue to pay through the nose.'

A DISGRUNTLED elector described a politician's election address as 'something that can be read between the letterbox and the waste-paper basket'.

AN MP who told a government Whip that he was at his 'wits' end' received the immediate response: 'Well, you haven't had to travel far.'

A BACK-BENCHER said of one prominent Labour Cabinet minister that he could 'brighten up a room just by leaving it'.

THE TROUBLE with some of the big guns in politics is that they are of small calibre and are big bores.

ALL POLITICIANS are sincere – whether they mean it or not.

TONY BENN is the ideal person to be marooned on a desert island with, as he is the only person who could possibly justify cannibalism.

A POLITICIAN 'is someone who divides his time between running for office and running for cover'.

HEREDITARY PEER: 'An MP is someone who stands for what he believes others will fall for.'

'A POLITICIAN is a man who approaches every issue with an open mouth – generally with both feet stuffed inside.'

OVERHEARD IN the Strangers' Bar (known as 'The Kremlin'): 'I am sorry you didn't like my telling people at the party that Neil Kinnock is stupid. I had no idea it was a secret.'

ON EDWINA CURRIE: 'At Christmas, I would rather hang her and kiss the mistletoe'. And: 'She's so conceited I'm sure that she has her x-rays retouched.'

Said behind Edwina's back: 'I like her approach. Now let's see her departure.'

Again on Edwina: 'She may be thoughtless, but she's never speechless.'

Also on Edwina Currie: 'She's the kind of person who gives people something to live for – revenge.'

ON MILDRED GORDON: 'She's probably bought those clothes for a ridiculous figure – hers.'

ON ROBERT Maclennan: 'He might have had an idea once, but it died of loneliness.'

ON LABOUR MP Tommy Graham: 'He has so many chins he uses a bookmark to find his collar.'

ON DAVID Alton: 'I hear that they're making a study of his family tree. He must be the sap.'

ON NIGEL GRIFFITHS: 'He is smarter than he looks, but then again, he'd have to be.'

OVERHEARD ON Marion Roe: 'I like her new hairdo – did she arrive on a motorbike?'

AFTER A meeting of the Curry Club: 'Please breathe the other way. You're bleaching my hair.'

COMMENTS ON John Marek: 'The person who said: "All things must end" never heard him talk.'
  'Generally speaking, he is generally speaking.'

ANONYMOUS COMMENT on Ann Widdecombe MP: 'She has a nice sense of rumour.'

'IF A little bird whispered something in her ear, it must have been a cuckoo.'

'THERE ARE two reasons why my wife doesn't *mind* her own *business*. She has neither.'

'IF HE aims to please then he's a terrible shot.'

WHIP TO back-bencher: 'What's on your mind? – if you'll forgive the exaggeration.'

FORMER MP: 'The women in my constituency are so ugly, if they held a beauty contest no one would win.'

MUTTERINGS DURING a speech by MP Mildred Gordon: 'She may be as fit as a fiddle, but she looks more like a double bass to me.'

'Beauty isn't everything, but in her case it's nothing.'

SUPPORTING THE view expressed by Prince Charles: 'Most architects think by the inch, talk by the yard and deserve to be kicked by the foot.'

ON TERRY DICKS: 'He was born ignorant and he's been losing ground ever since.'

ON A 'rent-a-quote' MP: 'The only print he will leave on the sands of time will be heel-marks.'

ON A Whip: 'Some people are right-handed, some people are left-handed – he is just underhanded.'

'HIS EARS are bookends for a vacuum.'

ON NICHOLAS BENNETT, 'Good things may come in small packages, but so does poison.'

ON DENIS HEALEY: 'He's not really such a bad person, until you get to know him.'

'HE INTENDS to turn over a new leaf – let's hope it's poison ivy.'

'THE ONLY thing he ever took up at University was space.'

OVERHEARD ON Nick Soames: 'He can trace his ancestors back to royalty – King Kong.'

ON LABOUR MP Dennis Turner: 'How can he sing with feeling? If he had any he wouldn't sing.'

'I wouldn't say his voice is heavenly, although it is certainly unearthly.'

'OF COURSE I can take a joke – where do you want to go?'

OVERHEARD ON Norman Tebbit: 'If he bit his tongue he would die of acid poisoning.'

ON DENNIS SKINNER: 'The only thing bright about him is the seat of his pants.'

'Why has he never been on holiday? He doesn't need to – he's on one long ego trip.'

'HE HAS a clear mind – not cluttered up with facts.'

'DON'T APOLOGIZE. I've enjoyed talking to you. My mind needed the rest.'

ON PADDY ASHDOWN: 'The more I think of him – the less I think of him.'

'THE STORK that brought him should have been fined for smuggling dope.'

ON DAVID OWEN: 'It's amazing how many people who go around in circles think that they are a big wheel.'

'IF HE does have a sixth sense, all I can say is there's no sign of the other five.'

WHEN A back-bencher asked for a day away from the

Norman Tebbit

House because he would like to attend his mother-in-law's funeral, his Whip replied: 'So would I.'

AN MP struggling with a crossword: 'With what do you connect the name Baden-Powell?'
Government Whip: 'A hyphen.'

LOOKING AT an overweight female MP: 'Since the invention of elastic, throughout the world women must now take up one third less space.'

MP IN a bar at the House:'This beer is a bit cloudy.'
Barman (not known for his polite manner): 'What do you expect for a pound – thunder and lightning?'

BACK-BENCHER TO Party Whip: 'When two people agree on everything, only one of them is doing the thinking.'

A TORY MP once said, 'The Conservative Party is like a bird. It has a right wing and a left wing but its brains are in the middle.'

'THERE ARE a number of things wrong with Westminster. One of them is that everyone has been too long away from home.'

DURING THE cold War, a Conservative back-bencher said of Russian premier Khrushchev: 'Russia's ability to send a man to Mars would be a big step towards world peace – if they sent the right man.'

A FRENCH MEP talking to an Irish MEP after a heated debate said: 'Why is it that you Irish always fight for money while we French only fight for honour?'

'I think,' the Irishman replied, 'that each fights for what he lacks.'

ONE POLITICIAN defined a scandal as: 'A breeze stirred up by a couple of windbags.'

OVERHEARD DURING a debate on embryo research (about one of the leaders of the anti-abortion campaign): 'If she were just a little more narrow-minded, her right ear would be on the wrong side of her head.'

THE GOSSIP at Westminster revealed that one sacked member of Neil Kinnock's Shadow Cabinet said: 'You can send a message around the world in half a second and yet it seems to take years to force a simple idea through a quarter inch of human skull.'

ADVICE OVERHEARD from a government Whip to a new MP: 'The best way to save face is to keep the lower end of it shut.'

ON LIBERAL Cyril Smith: 'He would be brilliant if he retained as much of what he reads as of what he eats.'

FOLLOWING THE revelation that Labour MP Ron Brown had taken a female into the shower room at the House of Commons, and following a disastrous court case which resulted in his being deselected, a Tory back-bencher was overheard to say: 'He had a shower and then found he was all washed up.'

WHEN ONE Labour MP demanded to know where was the stumbling block to the adoption of a particular policy, he was told that Neil Kinnock covered it with his hat.

OVERHEARD IN a bar at the House of Commons, a Labour back-bencher commented on former Tory Party Chairman, Kenneth Baker: 'If he said what he thinks, he'd be speechless.'

A RESEARCH assistant expressed his concern to his employer MP that his constituents could not understand from the MP's speech what his view was on a particular subject. The MP responded: 'That *is* good! It took me a couple of hours to draft the speech so it had that effect.'

ON DR RHODES BOYSON MP: 'He looks like a character out of an unpublished novel by Charles Dickens.'

SOME POLITICIANS who change their views are accused of 'seeing the light'. If the truth were known, many of them have merely 'felt the heat'.

A LABOUR left-winger: 'You can say what you like about Kinnock – but God help you if you say what you don't like.'

A CONSERVATIVE campaigner was told the difficult task he would have mounting an election campaign against Neil Kinnock. 'After all, he is now a household name,' the man said.

'So what?' came the reply. 'So is shit.'

DURING THE Gulf conflict following Iraq's decision to invade Kuwait, many Britains and Americans were surprised by the lack of support shown by Britain's so-called European partners towards the efforts of the allied troops. This led to the jibe at Westminster: 'What is the difference between a piece of buttered toast and the rest of Europe?' asked one MP. The response came without hesitation: 'You can make soldiers out of a piece of toast.'

Insults against the Irish have been around for many years and the Gulf War generated two new ones. One Conservative MP proudly announced to his colleagues that it had just been on the news that the Irish had developed a new parachute for use in the Gulf . . . 'It opens on impact.'

Another Irish joke involved the story that they had sent two cargo ships to the Gulf to help the allies. The allied commander was amazed to discover that the first ship was merely full of sand and the second ship contained powdered cement. Baffled by this rather odd cargo, he asked the Irish captain the purpose of carrying such a strange load and received the reply: 'It's ammunition to help you with the war effort.'

Still baffled, the allied commander enquired 'Ammunition?'

'Yes' the Irish captain responded. 'Didn't you say that you were intending to carry out a mortar attack?'

GLOSSARY

The readiness of politicians to abuse each other has, over the years, led to a number of new words entering the vocabulary. The following list contains some of the words which have found their way into the dictionary as a result of political invective.

APPEASER 'One who placates or settles' from the Old French *à* and *pais* peace. Until the premiership of Neville Chamberlain (1937–40), the words, 'appease', 'appeasement' and 'appeaser' were basically neutral. It was after the failure of his policy towards Hitler – often described by Chamberlain himself as 'a method of appeasement' – that this word became regarded as a form of criticism. Now it is often used to insult anyone who seems ready to abandon his principles to mollify a third party. Thus, Conservative MPs frequently refer to Socialists as 'appeasing the trade unions'. Similarly, Labour MPs have from time to time referred to Conservatives as seeking to 'appease their paymasters in British industry'.

BACKSTABBER 'A false friend.' This expression is quite a recent one, being traced back to the year 1906, when it was used in the *Westminster Gazette*. 'I will tell you my idea of a false friend and backstabber – to sweat the workmen for a personal profit and fawn on them for political profit, to promise old age pensions for votes and having got the votes to refuse them.' Used by an MP when referring to an unreliable colleague on his own side of the House.

BUNKUM This word, often used to describe a speech by a politician, means 'claptrap'. The word originally was used to mean an insincere political speech made only for the purpose of impressing one's constituents. The original spelling appears to have been 'buncombe', and originated from a speech made by Congressman Felix Walker, who represented North Carolina in the United States Congress. He insisted on making a long-winded and showy speech during the debate on the Missouri question apparently on the sole grounds that the people who inhabited a town in his constituency called 'Buncombe' expected a speech from him. Today, some journalists would argue the word could describe any political speech! In the United States, the word has been abbreviated even further to 'bunk'.

BUREAUCRAT 'A public servant.' Originally the word was descriptive and not insulting, but modern-day usage has the connotation of paper shuffler or penpusher. The word dates from the mid-nineteenth century and appears to derive from the word bureau – a writing desk.

BURKE 'To suffocate or suppress.' The word appears to have come into use after the activities of William Burke, who was hanged in 1829. Together with William Hare, he enticed men back to a lodging house in Edinburgh, got them drunk, then suffocated them in order to sell their bodies for medical research. After being arrested, Hare made a full confession and Burke was sent to the gallows.

CARPET-BAGGER 'A political outsider who stands for election in a constituency in which he has no previous interest or connection.' The word appears to be of American origin, the carpet bag having been a symbol for gentlemen who travelled light, particularly bankers, with no permanent local residence, few possessions and who had a way of disappearing when most wanted. The word was popularized just after the American Civil War as a term of abuse for northerners who moved south for political and financial gain. (US public documents published in 1868 contain the comment: 'I would sooner trust the black man than the white scallywag or carpet-bagger.')

CHAUVINIST 'Excessive devotion to one's sex or to one's race.' Popularized in the 1970s, particularly in the phrase 'male chauvinist pig'. The word originally appears to have meant someone who was excessively patriotic. It comes from the surname of Nicholas Chauvin, who was a soldier so excessively devoted to Napoleon that he became a laughing-stock, first to his regiment and then to the nation at large, his name being used to describe a flag-waving character in French music-hall performances during the last century.

CODSWALLOP 'Nonsense or rubbish.' The origin is apparently unknown but appears to be a derivative of 'cod', which is an old word for describing a small bag. (Thus 'codpiece', the bag-like garment worn by men in the Middle Ages to cover the opening in the front of their trousers or hose – and frequently padded for special effect.) Cod has also been used as a slang word for testicles. Probably, in its original use, the word was therefore not heard in polite circles.

COON 'An insulting description for a black person, with racialist overtones.' The word is North American and in the early nineteenth century had no racialist overtones but was used to describe a Whig politician. It appears to be a shortening of the word 'raccoon' (early Whig Party parades in the United States featured live raccoons as well as coon skins). The word retained this use until towards the end of the last century, when the racial sense of the word was developed by a hit song of 1896 'All Coons Look Alike to Me', which was performed by one Ernest Hogan who himself was black. The insult was revived in the late 1960s and early 1970s, particularly by frequent use on television by Johnny Speight's creation Alf Garnett.

CRAP 'A coarse slang word for rubbish.' It appears to be almost a euphemism for the even coarser 'shit'. Frequently used in the USA to describe the arguments of an opponent. It appears to have developed in the nineteenth century when the slang expressions 'crapping cases' and 'crapping castles' were used to describe lavatories.

CURMUDGEON A word that is not in current use in Britain, but which means a grumpy person who has some redeeming qualities. Although the word sounds like an Old English insult, it was used frequently to describe Harold Ickes, who was Secretary of the Interior during the first year of Truman's Presidency. He was called 'the old curmudgeon' so often that he adopted the insult when he wrote *Autobiography of a Curmudgeon* in 1943. The word was in use much earlier than that, and appears in some of Samuel Johnson's writings.

CLAPTRAP This word appears to originate in the early nineteenth century, when it was first used to describe the 'showy language of politicians intended to attract applause' (a speech intended to 'trap' the 'clap'). The word is now used to describe inaccurate, empty or misleading words.

DEADBEAT An American word used frequently by politicians of each other and meaning 'a worthless person; a loafer'. It dates from the latter half of the last century.

DEMAGOGUE The original meaning of this word was 'a popular orator or leader'. Today, it is a term used primarily of politicians who are obsessed with a particular issue. (In America, the word has even been used as a verb 'the Democrats are making a mistake by demagoguing this issue' – Labour Secretary Bill Brock commenting in 1986).

DO-GOODER 'A well-meaning but soft-headed person with a social conscience.' This phrase developed its current insulting political sense in the early part of this century in Britain.

DOPE 'A stupid person.' The word may have derived from the slang word for drugs to refer to someone who behaved as under the influence of cocaine or heroin. The word developed during the middle of the last century as a form of insult. American publisher William Loeb used it in his description of President Eisenhower. (His obituary said: 'He called President Eisenhower a dope and Senator Eugene McCarthy a skunk.')

DOUBLE-CROSSER 'A cheat who cheats other cheaters.' The phrase was popularized in the middle of the last century by politicians and also by US gamblers and thus entered the language.

DOVE 'Someone who favours diplomacy to obtain peace rather than risk war.' The opposite of hawk. Doves and hawks use each other's names derisively of each other. Although the dove is an ancient symbol of peace, in politics the word has only been widely in use this century, particularly since the Second World War.

DRY 'A right-winger.' A word whose political use originated in Britain to describe those who support the economic policies of Margaret Thatcher – her opponents being called wets.

EGGHEAD An insulting term for 'an intellectual'. The word was popularized as a rather snide term for an intellectual during the 1952 American Presidential campaign, when it was used as a criticism of Adlai Stevenson. Stevenson himself tried to brush off the insult by responding: 'eggheads of the world unite, you have nothing to lose but your yokes.'

EXTREMIST Someone who is 'not a moderate', usually a politician, and almost always used as an insult whether referring to a left-winger or a right-winger. Only one major politician in the world has dared to encourage the view that he was an extremist in recent times and that was Barry Goldwater who, when accepting the Republican Party's presidential nomination in 1964 said, in response to attacks that he was an extremist: 'Extremism in the defence of liberty is no vice . . . and let me tell you that moderation in the pursuit of justice is not a virtue.' The ploy did not work. He lost the election.

EYEWASH Another word for 'nonsense', with the insulting implication that there is an attempt to flatter or fool the audience. The word dates from the end of the last century. Similar to 'hogwash'. English in origin.

FASCIST 'A doctrinaire and authoritarian politician, usually, but not necessarily, of the right.' The origin of this word appears to be Benito Mussolini's fascist government of Italy (1922–43). The word has gradually achieved a wider application and its use is not now confined merely to insulting politicians. Police officers at demonstrations are frequently referred to by left-wing agitators as 'fascist pigs'.

FIFTH-COLUMNIST 'A traitor or someone whose loyalty is in doubt and who may be engaging in subversive behaviour.' The phrase originates from the Spanish Civil War, following remarks made by General Molar when he stated that he was counting on 'four columns of troops outside Madrid and another column of persons hiding within the city'. The phrase 'fifth column' appeared in the Press the next day.

FLUNKEY 'A servant'. The word appears to date from the late eighteenth century and is Scots in origin, but is frequently used in politics by the Eastern bloc as an insulting way of describing allies of the United States ('pro-American flunkeys').

FREELOADER 'A sponger.' Someone who lives it up, usually eating or drinking at another's expense. A very recent word dating from about the time of the Second World War and American in origin. Frequently used about politicians in the States, but an insult that has not really caught on yet in Britain.

GOBBLEDYGOOK 'Incomprehensible words or writing.' A frequent insult to government drafting of legislation. The word is a recent invention of American Congressman Mr Maverick who, during the Second World War, issued an order banning 'gobbledygook language' and instructed those under his employ: 'Say clearly what you're talking about.' The word caught on immediately and is in regular use on both sides of the Atlantic.

GOVERNOR OF MASSACHUSETTS Someone who is not liked and who is regarded as a bit of a bighead. Not in use outside the United States. This was a phrase used frequently during the 1988 Presidential election campaign by George Bush. His constant references to Michael Dukakis by his title 'Governor of Massachusetts', rather than by his own name, was a clever and effective put-down.

GUTTERSNIPE 'A disreputable person.' The word dates from the mid-nineteenth century and has frequently been used by politicians, but today seems to have fallen somewhat into disuse. Winston Churchill called Hitler 'a bloody guttersnipe', while across the Atlantic President Harry Truman said of music critic Paul Hume, 'A guttersnipe is a gentleman compared to you.'

HACK 'A writer for hire, but has insulting connotations.' Usually a whore, or a tired writer whose work reflects his condition. The word is a shortening of hackney and stems from the days when hackney horses were rented out. Originally the phrase came to mean a poor horse. Today the word has also been extended to include politicians (eg party hacks). (The reference to hack writers has also produced the word 'hackneyed'.)

HASH 'A mess.' This meaning dates back to the first part of the eighteenth century. The phrase 'to settle one's hash' – meaning to silence, or bring to account, goes back to the nineteenth century. Frequently used to insult politicians. Insults thrown at Ronald Reagan were described as 'an old tired reheated hash' by his Secretary of Education, William J Bennett, in 1987.

HATCHET-MAN 'Someone who launches vicious attacks upon others.' Mainly used to describe a politician who takes on the unpleasant task of insulting the opposition. In America Senator Bob Dole has been described as the Republican's 'hatchet-man' due to his acerbic tongue. In the nineteenth century, the phrase was used to describe the Chinese who were hired to commit murders in the United States.

HAWK (*see* Dove) 'Someone who thinks that international differences are resolved properly through the display of military strength.'

HENCHMAN 'A trusted servant or adherent', particularly in politics, who does the dirty work for his leader (similar to hatchet-man).

HOGWASH 'Nonsense.' Frequently used to describe an opposition politician's speech. A rather insulting way of saying 'rubbish'.

HYPE 'A deception, particularly in terms of someone promoting the deception through inflated words or high-pressure selling'. This word appears to date to the aftermath of the First World War and was popularized by the record industry with reference to the use of high-pressure sales tactics to see that a record or a particular piece of sheet music reached the charts. In politics, it has been used frequently and was a favourite word of Ronald Reagan, who criticized the peace movement: 'Peace is a beautiful word but those who abuse it are engaged in a campaign of modern hype.'

IMPERIALIST 'A person or country who argues that a nation's powers and influence should be extended beyond its borders'. The word has been used particularly by the Eastern bloc to insult capitalists and suggest they are intent on extending their borders. A favourite insult used by the USSR to describe Britain or America was to describe them as 'imperialist and aggressive nations'.

LEFT 'A radical, usually a left-winger or Liberal.' Almost

exclusively used as a political insult by conservatives to imply that someone is a Communist sympathizer. ('Left-winger.')

LIAR 'Untruthful person.' A taboo word in the British House of Commons. The most commonly used insult between politicians and yet it is not allowed in the Mother of Parliaments. In the House of Commons, euphemisms are often used to call someone a liar, such as alleging that an opponent is being 'economical with the truth'.

MACHIAVELLIAN 'Cunning, unscrupulous and deceitful.' A word derived from the name of Niccolo Machiavelli, who was regarded as a clever but evil person. Always at least one member of the UK government Whip's office is invariably so described.

MAVERICK 'Someone who is independently minded and is something of a loner.' The word is American in origin and seems to emanate from a description of Samuel A Maverick, a Texas rancher who neglected to brand many of his cattle. However, by the latter part of the last century, the word was used, particularly of politicians, to describe someone who disobeyed party discipline and 'did his own thing'.

NOSEY PARKER 'Someone who pries or snoops into the business of others.' It appears that the phrase arose following the behaviour of a former Archbishop of Canterbury, one Matthew Parker, who kept close watch on what other people were doing.

OPPORTUNIST 'Someone who has sacrificed his principles for expediency.' Frequently used to criticize one's political opponents. The term was first being used during the nineteenth century in French politics, especially with reference to the supporters of Léon Gambetta.

PETAIN 'A dictator.' Derives from Marshal Pétain, who collaborated with the Germans as head of the French Vichy government during the Second World War.

QUISLING 'A traitor.' Derives from the role of Major Quisling, a Norwegian Nazi leader who helped the Germans conquer his country during the Second World War. A word disallowed in parliamentary debate in the parliament of the United Kingdom.

RADICAL 'Rather extreme.' A form of political insult. The term appears to have entered the political arena with the Radical Reform Movement in the late eighteenth century. In the United States of America, the term was originally associated with Socialists and others on the left in politics.

REACTIONARY 'Someone who responds to a situation by moving in the opposite direction.' In political terms, it is used to mean someone who is an opponent of revolution or of progressive moves. The word dates from the mid-nineteenth century and carries with it an insulting sense of backwardness and unwillingness to apply modern ideas to current problems.

ROGUE ELEPHANT An insulting phrase which means 'a person who is something of a loner and prone to violent outbursts'. It was used by Tory back-bencher John Wilkinson to describe Cabinet minister, Michael Heseltine, immediately after his resignation when he stormed out of a Cabinet meeting and told the policeman on the door at Number 10 Downing Street: 'I've resigned.'

SCAB 'A worker who refuses to join a trade union or

who works while others are on strike.' The word has been an insult since William Shakespeare's day, but the use to describe strike-breakers seems to have arisen in the latter part of the last century.

SLACKER 'One who shirks work or evades obligations.' The word is quite recent and dates from the end of the last century. It was popularized during the First World War by patriotic politicians who applied it to conscientious objectors and pacifists and others who appeared reluctant to support the war effort.

THROTTLEBOTTOM 'A bumbling and incompetent politician.' The word is American in origin, the term comes from Vice-President Alexander Throttlebottom who was a fictional character in the musical *Of Thee I Sing*, written in 1931. The original production starred George Murphy, a dancer, who later became a Republican Senator. The word is still in use today in the United States, and was applied to Vice-President Dan Quayle during the 1988 election.

TINPOT (AND TINHORN) 'An inferior contemptible person, especially a politician.' The phrase 'tinpot politician' originated in Britain during the latter half of the last century to mean someone who was cheap, poor, shabby, or worthless. The phrase caught on in the USA, where they improved it somewhat by changing tinpot to tinhorn. The phrase is also used of gamblers.

TROGLODYTE Originally the word meant 'a cave-dweller', but in modern usage, particularly in the United States, it means an extreme right-winger. Today not in popular use in Britain.

WET 'A left-wing Conservative.' Appears to have originated from the description given to her opponents in the Conservative Party by Margaret Thatcher in the early 1980s.

WINDBAG 'A person who talks a lot, especially one who doesn't know what he is talking about.' The word seems to have first been used in the nineteenth century and may have developed from the windbag, or bellows, of an organ. In modern times, it is frequently applied to politicians of all parties but particularly to describe Neil Kinnock. It is in use in the United States as well.

WOWSER 'Someone who is puritanical, especially a kill-joy'. The word originated in Australia during the latter half of the last century. Not in general use in Britain, it is nevertheless used in some parts of the globe. In 1970, Canadian Prime Minister Pierre Trudeau said, during a visit to Australia: 'You have wowserism – we have Toronto.'

INDEX

217

Index